Pages From The Past

Thirty years of Victorian life in the *Beverley Guardian*

by
Paul A. Hesp and Peter H. Robinson

Pages From The Past is dedicated to the world of newspaper journalists, in particular those past and present of the *Beverley Guardian*, and especially those characters who 'made the news'.

© Text 1986   Paul A. Hesp and Peter H. Robinson
© Sketches 1986   Steve Oldfield
© Photographs 1986   Mark Ogden
ISBN 0 948929 05 7
Published by Highgate Publications (Beverley) Ltd.,
24 Wylies Road, Beverley, HU17 7AP
Telephone (0482) 866826

Printed by B.A. Press
2-4 Newbegin, Lairgate, Beverley, HU17 8EG
Telephone (0482) 882232

CONTENTS

THE PEOPLE INVOLVED IN *PAGES FROM THE PAST*

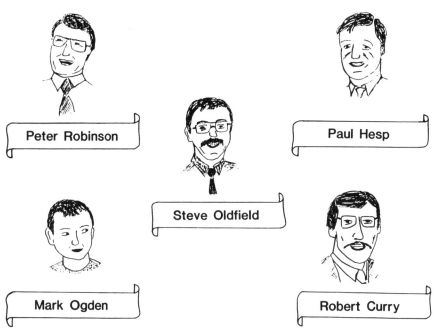

Peter Robinson

Paul Hesp

Steve Oldfield

Mark Ogden

Robert Curry

BRITISH CURRENCY CONVERSION CHART

*DECIMAL CURRENCY
New pence

OLD MONEY (PRE 1971)
Pounds, shillings and pence

Old Money		Decimal Currency
¼d	Farthing	0·1p
½d	Ha'penny	0·21p
1d	Penny	0·42p
3d	Thrupenny bit	1·25p
6d	Sixpence	2·5p
1/-	Shilling (Twelve pennies)	5p
2/-	Florin (Two shillings)	10p
2/6	Half a Crown (Two shillings and sixpence)	12½ P
5/-	Crown (Five shillings)	25p
10/-	Ten shillings	50p
£1	Pound (Twenty shillings)	100p
1 gn	Guinea (Twenty one shillings)	105p

* Britain converted to decimal currency in 1971 on 15th February.

4

FOREWORD

When I was asked to pen the foreword to this book there was no book — just an idea, and, although I had no way of knowing how the idea would form, it was an opportunity I was not about to turn down. As the book progressed and the original idea saw many changes, so did my foreword. The book has been sectionalised by categories, and that means you can read your favourite items over and over again knowing exactly where they can be found, and believe me, you will have your favourites, just as much as I have mine. The book has been carefully researched and compiled from the 'best' stories of the day, many chosen because of the questions they raise (which give you something to think about), others because they reflect the period, and many more because of the wit and entertainment value they provide due to the way they have been reported (and if the *Beverley Guardian* ever runs out of items for their *From The Past* section I'm sure they'll be able to use items from this book). The illustrations throughout are there for four reasons: i. like my writing this foreword, it gave Steve Oldfield something useful to do. ii. they enhance the text. iii. they illustrate the wit I was just talking about, and possibly iv. if you can't read you can buy the book for the pictures. Hopefully, your enthusiasm for the subject will enable the 'second best' to go to publication in the near future.

Although compared to many residents I have only been living in the town for a short time (18 years), I was struck by the fact that, having seen many changes in the town over those years, many a parallel can be seen between incidents of over 100 years ago and today. This is yet another aspect of fascination the book has to offer, which just goes to prove some things never change — and although some people may say, 'Let bygones be bygones', translated as meaning, 'Let past troubles remain in the past' — this is one occasion when past troubles will provide good reading.

If you have an interest in life in the area during Victorian times, then this book is definitely for you.

Robert Curry
October, 1986

INTRODUCTION

The original idea for this project was conceived early in 1984, for it was then, whilst searching through old copies of the *Beverley Guardian* for my history of the Beverley Playhouse Cinema, that my eyes frequently strayed from the intended search towards other interesting items. I soon realised that not all nasty or unpleasant things belonged to the Eighties but had been going on for years.

My original project continued, and so did the times I slowed down to read old 'newsy' and 'juicy' bits with great fascination. This started me thinking that I would, some time in the future, like to compile a collection of the 'best of the worst' or a 'golden treasury of nasties'. Interest in the subject was fired further when I repeatedly heard my parents say, whilst gleaning the news from radio or television, that, 'It never used to be like that in our day, did it?' The answer from the other partner was invariably, 'No, never! People never did that sort of thing when we were kids.' I would remonstrate and try to describe or relate some of my 'nasty' press findings, but they always found some excuse or explanation that it was never as bad in those good old days as it is today.

And so the foundation for this project was laid, and on the afternoon of New Year's Eve, 1985, I joined forces with a colleague, Paul Hesp, to start the collection of material for our 'Nasties Collection'. Armed with a tape recorder, we progressed at great speed and within weeks we had amassed a wealth of interesting items, but, as happened on the Playhouse project, we both developed the straying eye, and just out of interest we taped many other items of appeal to us; some were little gems and so incredibly fascinating we just had to have them. The project now took a slightly different angle as we collected health and beauty tips, home care hints, and many more to complement our 'nasties', but so many were absolute treasures that we became diverted ever more towards this new interest. After sixteen weeks of intense research our project was as complete as we felt we could make it, to provide the reader with an easy-to-read trip back to those good old days.

You will find that at the beginning of each section, or chapter, we have included a brief introduction as a sort of guide to content and occasionally you will discover after an entry we have made our own personal comments which may perhaps reflect your own thoughts. Throughout our book we have attempted to retain (in chronological order) as much of the original flavour as possible from those old and much valued *Beverley Guardians*, and in many cases where proceedings were taken against offenders, we thought it prudent to drop the surnames and/or addresses in an attempt to protect any surviving relatives from possible embarrassment at discovering a skeleton in the cupboard.

Instead of listing acknowledgements separately, I feel thanks are more sincere if included within my introduction. Firstly, to my co-author Paul

Hesp. When he said yes I don't think he knew what he was letting himself in for, but, being my assistant manager at the Playhouse Cinema, I'm sure he realised that when I set my sights I usually reach my target. Thanks, Paul. Robert Curry, another member of the Playhouse staff, did such a good job 'translating' the Playhouse project that he was again invited/volunteered as a natural for 'translating' our very original notes to presentable typed manuscript (and he also does a good foreword). Steve Oldfield has shared my involvement with the Playhouse Cinema for many years, and, as this project developed, I felt that a contribution from his artistic talents would be an asset. Steve was flattered and wasted no time in producing a superb collection of illustrations which just have that 'right' look about them, and certainly do much to enhance the text.

By now you must be wondering how many more cinema staff could possibly be involved. Well, we do have one ex-member, Mark Ogden, and, although working at the Hull Film Theatre now, we still regard him as staff. His contribution? The front cover. From my original design idea, Mark brought the cover to fruition through his expert photography and artwork. It's also the results of his photography you will find throughout the book. Another valued friend on this project has been Mr. Philip Brown of the Beverley Public Library. Once again, Philip shared his wealth of knowledge with us and deserves a special thank you. Our thanks also to the staff of the library who have once again proved invaluable in their co-operation throughout.

Of course, this book and these thanks would not be possible were it not for our dear old *Beverley Guardians*, for without them we would have no *Pages From The Past*. Here I wish to acknowledge with thanks the co-operation of Jeremy Ashcroft-Hawley, Group Editor of East Yorkshire Newspapers Ltd., who has helped us both professionally and with enthusiasm. Thank you again, Jeremy.

Now to probably the most important people of all to thank, the publishers, Highgate Publications, John Markham, Martyn and Irene Kirby, for their enthusiasm for the project, for without them we would have no book. Thanks to another friend who has made a considerable contribution to the project with supportive typing of manuscript. We also acknowledge the kind permission of Lever Brothers Limited to reproduce their advertisement for Lifebuoy Soap, and Beecham Group p.l.c, for the reproduction of their Elliman's Embrocation advertising block.

Please join us now for a journey through our *Pages From The Past*.

Peter Harvatt Robinson
October, 1986

ACCIDENTS

Our collection of accidents is from some of the more interesting ones available — not interesting for the type of accident, but in many cases because of where they occurred. As you read this section you will come across some places you may never have heard of. These were Beverley's industrial heritage and have long since gone. The Iron and Waggon Works (the Foundry) occupied a vast area in the region of 11 acres on either side of Mill Lane. Crathorne's Mill was a flour mill situated between the Barmston Drain and River Hull, the site eventually becoming part of the shipyard. The Tannery was frequently in the news, not for accidents, but for the constant problem of pollution and the numerous battles over that problem. It's sad but the battle is over; the Tannery eventually closed and with it hundreds of jobs went, but the drains and the river became cleaner and sweeter. These and other small businesses have now gone, as has the Hull-York Railway line. Sadly, this closed for passenger service on 29 November, 1965.

Although we realise that accidents of any description are void of humour, we feel that within this collection there are many which will make you smile, not directly at the accident but at the often very detailed and vivid way in which they were reported by the press. *PHR*

CART ACCIDENT — On Saturday evening last about six o'clock as Mr. Hardy of Bishop Burton was in a light spring cart driving a spirited grey galloway, he, when near the Foundry, happened to touch the animal on the ears with his whip, which caused it to run away. The horse proceeded along Wilbert Lane at a fearful pace, and, arriving in Butcher Row, one of the wheels caught the curb stone of the Angel Inn, which overturned the vehicle, breaking the shafts and doing other damage. The unfortunate driver was picked up in a state of insensibility, and conveyed to the surgery of R. G. Boulton, Esq., where it was found that he had sustained a fracture of the skull. In the course of the evening he was taken in a cab to his residence, accompanied by Mr. Boulton, under whose treatment he is gradually recovering. FEBRUARY 1858

ACCIDENT AT THE FOUNDRY — Between eleven and twelve o'clock on Wednesday morning last a serious accident happened to a man named John Jones, who was employed to attend to the engine belonging to the above establishment. It appears that he had gone up some steps and was about to walk on a plank over the boilers when he was spoken to by a fellow workman. On turning round to give an answer his foot slipped, and he was precipitated into the fire hole beneath, a distance of nearly nine feet. Assistance being at hand, the poor fellow was speedily extricated from his perilous position, but he was so severely cut and bruised about his side, shoulder, and head, besides bleeding profusely, that it was deemed necessary to convey him to his residence in Walker's Yard in a cart. T. Sandwith, Esq., was sent for, who found, in addition to the injuries above described, that one of his ribs was broken. The unfortunate man at present lies in a very precarious state, but it is hoped that, by the skilful treatment of his medical attendant, he will soon recover, as we understand that he has a wife and six children to provide for. FEBRUARY 1858

ACCIDENT — On Saturday evening last, two waggons, each drawn by three horses, the property of Mr. J. B. Lowther, merchant, of this town, were on their way home laden with timber. In coming down Etton Dykes Hill the middle mare in one of the teams fell and spun round, when the wheels of the waggon came over her head, and caused instant death. We understand that this is the third valuable horse Mr. Lowther has lost in the last two months. MAY 1860

MIRACULOUS ESCAPE — Yesterday afternoon, an accident, which might have been attended with serious consequences, occurred to Mr. Charles Bartle, tailor, of North Bar Street. It appears that he was on Westwood witnessing the training of the East York Militia, and was lying with several others upon the turf, about twenty yards in front of the regiment, which were drawn into line for the purpose of firing a volley. Either from excitement or confusion, one of the militiamen discharged his rifle with the ramrod in the barrel, the consequence being that the ramrod came into violent contact with the watch in Mr. Bartle's waistcoat pocket and rebounded. The watch was completely smashed, the vest torn, and the ramrod, when picked up, was found to be bent almost in the shape of the letter S. The only ill effects experienced by Mr. Bartle from the shock was a pain in his side, but, had it not been for his watch, which caused the ramrod to rebound, he would, in all probability, have lost his life. MAY 1862

RAILWAY ACCIDENT — On Wednesday morning a serious accident occurred to a woman named Woodward, a huckster, *[hawker]* residing in Hull, who nearly lost her life through her own recklessness. It appears that she was a passenger for Market Weighton by the new line and by some means neglected to alight at her place of destination. Finding out her mistake as the train was proceeding towards Shipton, she jumped from the carriage, and in the fall sustained a deep cut on the forehead besides other extensive injuries. It is supposed that she lay in that state upon the ground for about an hour, as she was picked up by a goods train and brought to Beverley. She was afterwards sent on to Hull under the charge of one of the porters, and we understand that she is now going on favourably.

MAY 1865

ACCIDENT — On Sunday last, a young man named John Titchener, belonging to the band of the East York Militia, was very much hurt by attempting to leap the fence that encloses New Walk. It appears that he slipped and fell with his thighs upon the spikes with which the chain is studded, lacerating them considerably. He was conveyed home in a cab, and attended by Mr. Geo. Earle, surgeon, under whose care he continues.

FEBRUARY 1868

ACCIDENT — On Thursday morning the railway gates that protect the crossing at Flemingate were run into by the train which passes through Beverley at 6.55, from Hull to York. It appears that the driver whistled as usual on turning the bend from the gravel pit, but no response was made by the gatekeeper. The driver continued to whistle, and also slackened speed. He kept on, however, thinking no doubt that, as he was going slowly, the gates might be open before he got up with them; but this was not the case, and the result was a collision. The first gate, which opens outwards, was merely thrown back with great force, the lamp on top being hurled a distance of several yards. The second gate, which opened inwards, was completely smashed, the iron work being doubled up as if it were but wire. The round hut, in which the gatekeeper sits, was also very much damaged. Fortunately no one was injured. The train was going so slowly that it was brought to a stand as soon as the mischief was done. It is stated that the gatekeeper had been mistimed, and was not up when the accident occurred. The gates at this crossing were run through by a coal train, on a foggy Sunday morning, a few years ago. JUNE 1868

ACCIDENT — A youth named Foster, an apprentice to Mr. Jno. Stamford, builder, had his hand injured the other day through an explosion of gun powder. The accident occurred in the saddle room where he let some grains of powder drop on the still heated cinders, and this caused the cannister to burst. AUGUST 1871

ACCIDENT — The other day Mr. Charles Crickmer, son of the Rev. W. B. Crickmer, accidentally shot himself in the left hand with a pistol. The middle finger had to be amputated, and the sufferer is going on well towards recovery. NOVEMBER 1877

FALL FROM A HOUSE TOP — On Wednesday afternoon Mr. Cook, chimney sweep, ascended the roof of the house occupied by Mr. Goldham in Saturday Market, for the purpose of sweeping a chimney from the outside. By some means the ladder on the tiles slipped and he fell into the street below, alighting on his hip. He was conveyed home and attended by Mr. Appleton and Mr. Park, who found him suffering from severe injuries, the extent of which are scarcely at present known. DECEMBER 1877

FALL DOWN A WELL — Miraculous Escape — A woman in the service of Mrs. Cook, of St. Mary's Terrace, had an extraordinary escape last night week. It seems that she had been wandering about amongst some buildings in course of erection in Westwood Road, and whilst so doing fell into a well which had been left uncovered. Although she fell a distance of about fifty feet, she was alive when found, and was groping about at the bottom, which was dry. Her cries reached the ears of Mrs. Cook, and some of the workmen at the houses, who lodged with the latter, went in search of the woman and found her as described. Owing to the depth of the well it was some time before she could be extricated. When brought to the top it was found that her head was cut in two or three places, but she was otherwise uninjured. Dr. Appleton was called, and he attended to her wounds. At the bottom of the well were brick ends and broken bottles, and the only wonder is she was found alive. SEPTEMBER 1878

ACCIDENT AT A TAN YARD — On Thursday morning a bag of gambia [gambier — a gum used in tanning] fell upon a workman named James Conley, employed by Messrs. Hodgson's works, causing severe internal injuries. He was taken at once to the Cottage Hospital, and attended by Dr. Thompson, and is now progressing favourably.
MARCH 1880

SAD ACCIDENT TO AN OLD MAN — On Monday last, as nothing had been seen of William Spence, an inmate of one of the Bede Houses, the police forced an entrance into his residence and found him lying at the foot of the stairs, into which position he had fallen on the previous night. He was very much bruised about the head and considerably shaken. He was conveyed to the Cottage Hospital, where he has received every attention. Mr. Spence, who we believe is 85 years of age, was for a long time in the service of the Corporation as one of the scavengers.   MARCH 1881

(So, the Corporation employed scavengers, did they? Being curious, I looked it up, and according to my Collins Dictionary found that a scavenger is 'one employed in cleaning streets, removing refuse, etc.,' also, and as I had originally thought, 'an animal which feeds on carrion'.)

DISTRESSING FATALITY TO A BEVERLEY MAN — A navvy employed on the Scarborough and Whitby Railway works at Scarborough has succumbed to injuries sustained in a singular manner. To enable the deceased, whose name was William Slater of Beverley, to climb up a small embankment out of the way of an approaching locomotive a fellow workman stuck his pick into the soil for the deceased to take hold of, but the point unfortunately caught and entered the man's hand. Erysipelas supervened, and death resulted on Tuesday. At an inquest held in Scarborough Town Hall on Wednesday night a verdict in accordance with these facts was returned.   APRIL 1883

ACCIDENT ON THE RAILWAY — Yesterday evening week, Charles Wake, one of the post office employees, had a narrow escape at the railway station. He was crossing the rails with a parcels hamper when the buffer of an advancing engine struck him and knocked him into the six foot. One of his arms was considerably injured and his system received a severe shock.

MARCH 1884

CHRISTMAS TOYS.

A SPLENDID ASSORTMENT of CHRISTMAS TOYS.—Leotards and others in endless variety. New Games, Acrobats, Pharaoh's Serpents, &c. Now ready for inspection, at MRS. KING'S, Toy Warehouse, Market Place, Beverley.

CHRISTMAS TOYS! CHRISTMAS TOYS!

A LARGE assortment of Christmas Tree Articles at MRS. FOWLER'S, Toll Gavel.

WANTED, HOUSEMAIDS and GENERAL SERVANTS, at once.—Mrs. IRELAND, Register Office, St. Mary's Terrace, Beverley. 232

A CARD.—TO ALL WHO ARE SUFFERING FROM THE errors and indiscretions of youth, nervous weakness, early decay, loss of manhood, &c., I will send a receipt that will cure you, FREE OF CHARGE. This great remedy was discovered by a missionary in South America. Send a self-addressed envelope to the REV. JOSEPH T INMAN, *Station D New York City, U.S.A.* 150

JOHN WALKER,

HOSIER, GLOVER, HATTER, and FURRIER, Market-Place, Beverley, is in immediate want of an APPRENTICE.

W A N T E D

A GROOM, to take charge of Two Horses and a Carriage, and wait at Table. A Married Man to sleep at his own home will be preferred.

Apply to R. LOFTUS, Cabinet Maker, North Bar Street, Beverley.

ADVERTISEMENTS

Something to sell? A situation vacant? Lost, found or wanted? These are a few of the headings you can expect to find in practically every newspaper today. But have you ever given a thought to what occupied those columns around a hundred years ago? Just in case you have wanted to know what jobs were available and what folks wanted or had for sale, allow us to satisfy your curiosity as you read through our selection of 'The Best of the Ads', all from the Beverley Guardian *of those years gone by.*

As will be realised, there were thousands of adverts available to choose from, so we set about selecting those that reflected the period best. Some with a degree of humour, we are sure, quite unintentionally, but they made us laugh. In some cases it could have been our minds that read too much into them. We have included many of our favourites and hope you will find this section both interesting and amusing, but remember: all the ads are a long way out of date, so please resist the temptation to reply to any.

PHR

NEW LARD WANTED — NEWSTEAD & CO. will give 9¼d per lb for New Lard, in Bladders, delivered at their Establishment.
MARKET PLACE, BEVERLEY. NOVEMBER 1856

HOUSE KEEPER WANTED — In a farm house, near Beverley, where the family is small. A person of middle age would be preferred. Character required.
APPLY AT the *Guardian* Office.   JANUARY 1860

WANTED — A situation as Brewer; accustomed to ale, porter, and bitter beer, and also to stone square brewing. Apply to William Briggs, at the Steam Brewery, Ladygate, Beverley. Five years reference to character.
JANUARY 1860

PAPER HANGINGS — A choice selection, from one halfpenny to sixpence per yard. House painting, Graining, Gilding, &c. J. SHAW, North Bar Street, Beverley.   AUGUST 1860

HORSE SINGEING BY GAS — Thomas Nicholson respectfully announces that he has engaged spacious premises in the yard of Mr. Jebson, veterinary surgeon, Ladygate, where he intends to take in horses to singe, and feels confident, from his long experience, that he will be able to finish all horses trusted to his care in an expeditious manner, and for neatness not to be surpassed, if equalled, by anyone in Beverley or the neighbourhood.
NOVEMBER 1860

WANTED from 10 to 15cwt of RANCID (genuine) LARD, for use in the manufacture of sheep ointment
Apply to C. HOBSON, BEVERLEY.   DECEMBER 1860

TO BE LET OUT, a neat HORSE and DOG CART.
Apply to G. Ward, Cross Keys Hotel.   FEBRUARY 1865

WANTED, by a widow lady, residing in Beverley, a middle-aged, attractive, cheerful person, as a general servant; references required. —
Address F.F., *Guardian* Office, Beverley.   AUGUST 1865

BEVERLEY GAS WORKS — Stokers wanted for the above — wages 24s per week.
Apply at the works, on or before Wednesday, 3rd January, 1866.
JOHN FOXALL, Manager.   DECEMBER 1865

WANTED a STOUT ACTIVE YOUTH, about 14 or 16 years old, to assist a GARDENER constantly in Gentleman's Garden.
Apply — Mr Browsho, Toll Gavel, Beverley.   JANUARY 1869

WANTED a GENERAL SERVANT, in a small house in the country, where a boy is kept. Wages £14 a year, and everything found.
Apply to Mrs. HUGH WYNDHAM, Wawne Cottage, Beverley.
MARCH 1869

LOST, out of the Cattle Train on Thursday last, DRAPE COW. Whoever will restore the same to Mr. T. Dunning, Kings Head Inn, Beverley, will have all expenses paid.   MAY 1869

TO BE SOLD CHEAP — A VERY LARGE BELL, Weighing 126lbs., AT DALE & SON'S, Ironmongers, Beverley.   DECEMBER 1869

If the party who took a PIG TROUGH out of a yard in Wood Lane does not return it, they will be prosecuted, as they are known.   FEBRUARY 1870

WANTED a FAMILY WASHING, in the Country.
Apply to Mrs Hall, Woodmansey.   FEBRUARY 1870

To Let Three acres of FOG. Apply to Mr. ROBT. UNDERWOOD, Willow Grove.   NOVEMBER 1870

(If, like me, the reader is unfamiliar with the land and thought that a printer's error had occurred and FOG should have read BOG, the solution is at hand, for, according to my Collins Dictionary, the definition of FOG is as follows: FOG n, growth of coarse grass after hay has been cut. FOG n, thick mist; watery vapour in the lower atmosphere; a cloud of dust or smoke obscuring visibility.)

LOST — On the 25th *ult.*, either in Westwood or Molescroft Road, a small TELESCOPE. The finder will be rewarded on leaving it at the *Guardian* office. SEPTEMBER 1871

WANTED an intelligent YOUTH, who writes a good hand, about fifteen years of age, in an office in Beverley.
Apply to A.B., at the *Guardian* office. SEPTEMBER 1872

FARM LABOURER wanted, who can milk, and to work on Farm. Wages 18s. a week and House. Apply to MR. JAMES DAWSON, Beverley.
JUNE 1874

WANTED a strong active Boy, not less than 14 years of age, to CLEAN BOOTS and KNIVES and make himself generally useful.
Apply at the *Guardian* office. FEBRUARY 1875

LOST between the Market Place and Beckside, on Thursday night, between seven and eight o'clock, HALF A SOVEREIGN, in a piece of paper. Particulars at the *Guardian* office. MAY 1875

WANTED, at Martinmas, a MARRIED FOREMAN, to meat the men. Character from last employer required. Apply — *Guardian* office.
OCTOBER 1875

(The spelling in this ad is as printed — a foreman who had to 'meat' his men, provided them with meals.)

SAINT MARY'S CHURCH — WANTED, TWO BELLOWS BLOWERS for Saint Mary's Church Organ from the 1st January next. The salary will be £5 a year each. Applications to be made to FREDERICK HOBSON. Lairgate, Beverley. DECEMBER 1875

WANTED — A young man to join another in a sitting room; separate bedrooms; near to Station, Beverley. — Apply *Guardian* Office, Beverley.
MAY 1876

The person who took the LADDER from Mr SCRUTON'S STACK, in Queensgate Road, a short time ago, will oblige by returning it at once.
AUGUST 1876

LOST — On the high road between Skidby and Beverley Minster, a MEERSCHAUM CIGAR HOLDER with Amber Mouthpiece, and a leather CIGAR CASE. Anyone finding the same will be rewarded on applying to H.H., 11, Blanket Row, Hull.
JANUARY 1877

LOST — On Tuesday, 29th May, between the White Horse Inn, Beverley, and Routh, a PURSE, containing TWO £5 Notes and £1 in Gold, also some memorandums. A reward of £3 will be paid to any person returning the same to F. Burrell, Beverley. The Notes are Stopped.
JUNE 1877

6th EAST YORK RIFLE VOLUNTEERS. — THERE are Vacancies for a few Young Men in this company, who can be enrolled and furnished with uniform, arms and accoutrements, gratis, on application to Sergeant-Major Smith, at the Head Quarters, Toll Gavel.
H. E. SILVESTER, Captain.
N.B. — All the travelling and necessary expenses of members are paid out of the funds of the Corps.
JANUARY 1879

LOST ON THURSDAY, January 30th, a little BLACK BITCH, with long Hair and White Mark on the Breast. Anyone bringing the Same to William Brown, Leven, or letting him know of its whereabouts, will be rewarded.
(That's no way to describe a lady.)
FEBRUARY 1879

MRS WYNN CORSET MAKER, VICAR LANE, BEGS to Call the attention of ladies to her CORSETS OF SUPERIOR SHAPE and QUALITY.
MARCH 1880
(Here we would like to direct the interested reader to our Health and Beauty section, July 1886, in an effort to encourage corset users to think carefully about this habit that can be as difficult to break as the habit of alcohol and tobacco with men.)

WANTED a steady honest MAN TO MILK six cows and sell milk. Wage and Commission from 18s. to 24s. per week. Apply, JOHN SOWEN, Keld Gate. JULY 1880

TAKEN from the Beverley Flower Show, a GLASS VASE. Whoever took it will please return it to the *Guardian* office. JULY 1880

A REWARD is offered for the discovery of the person who, a day or two ago, shot with a catapult and maimed a valuable Antwerp CARRIER PIGEON, belonging to W. Green, *Guardian* Office, Beverley; and it is also notified that persons found shooting at or molesting any pigeons, the property of Mr. Green, will be prosecuted. FEBRUARY 1881

FOUND in Swinemoor Lane, Beverley, on Friday, May 6th, a Red and White Fresh YOUNG COW. The owner can have the same, by paying all reasonable expenses, on applying to P. MUSGRAVE, Valiant Soldier Inn, Beverley Cattle Market. MAY 1881

ST. MARY'S CHOIR — WANTS BOYS with good voices and good characters, for the above choir. £3 a year given to Solo Boys. — Apply immediately to the vicar. JANUARY 1883

Perforated Toilet Paper in rolls should be in every household; prevents stoppage of drains; economical and neat. — Of all chemists, stationers, hairdressers. MARCH 1884

(No doubt cheering news for many. At last an end to newsprint? Certainly takes the bind out of paperwork.)

LOST a RED TURBIT PIGEON — Any person returning the same to Mr. T. S. Stephenson, Newbegin, Beverley, will be rewarded. MARCH 1884

BEVERLEY MINSTER — WANTED, a man as ASSISTANT SEXTON: Churchman under 40, able to mow the grass, manage the stoves, and clean the church. Wages £1 a week. Apply to the vicar or the churchwardens.   JUNE 1884
(To clean the church as well and for only £1!)

LOST, on Tuesday afternoon, Small Green CHEQUE for £3. Payment stopped. — Finder rewarded on returning same to *Guardian* Office, Beverley.   JULY 1885

LEFT, in St. Mary's church, on Sunday, September 19th, a BLACK FUR TIPPET. — The owner can have it by applying to the vestry room.
                                                                                OCTOBER 1885

WANTED, A man to catch the moles, for the parishes of Leconfield and Arram, containing 3,500 acres. — Apply stating terms to Robert Fisher, 229.   JANUARY 1886

WANTED — Ladies Requiring Servants, or Servants requiring Situations, Can be quickly supplied at Mrs. Crombie's, Market Place Beverley. N.B. — Special hirings on Saturdays.   FEBRUARY 1886

WANTED, to purchase *The Times*, day or two days after date of publication. — Green and Son, Newsagent, Beverley. FEBRUARY 1886 *(Obviously they hadn't heard about the perforated toilet paper in rolls — it had been available for almost two years. See advert MARCH 1884.)*

WANTED, EMIGRATION TO QUEENSLAND — Female domestic servants are in great demand, and receive wages varying from £20 to £50 per annum with board and lodging. Applicants must be between 17 and 35 years of age, and of good character. Free passages are granted by steamers from Blackwall, London, every fortnight on payment of £1 for ship kit. For forms of application apply to the Agent General for Queensland, 1 Westminster Chambers, Victoria Street, London SW. FEBRUARY 1886

WANTED, A single man as yard man, must be a good milker and understand the bringing up of calves. — Address 425, The *Guardian* Office, Beverley. MARCH 1886

FOUND — Left in the passage of the Assembly Rooms, Thursday, March 4th, 1886, an UMBRELLA. The owner can have it by paying expenses and applying to Mrs. Kilvington, 14 Hen Fields, Beverley. MARCH 1886

WANTED — Respectable washerwoman, copper and machine for use. — Apply, Mrs. Hick, Queensgate Road. MARCH 1886

WANTED — The public to know that the *Beverley Guardian* is the best paper in the East Riding for local, district, general news, and for advertising purposes. — Offices, Market Place, Beverley. MARCH 1886

LOST, between New Walk and Newbegin, a diamond out of a ring. — One pound reward if returned to the *Guardian* Office. JUNE 1886

WANTED, A good general servant, about 18 or 20, one from the Country preferred. — Apply, 20, Railway Street, Beverley. JUNE 1886

FOR SALE Small organ for sale, 4 stops. Suitable for school or mission room. — Apply F. Duncan, Keldgate, Beverley. JUNE 1886

ALCOHOL
(THE CUP THAT CHEERS!)

I remember my dear old Grandma saying, 'When drink's in, wit's out.' At the time I don't think I was old enough to sip from 'the cup that cheers'. However, there have been many occasions when I have not 'sipped' but 'supped' well from that cup, and I'm sure every time have said never again, or again! or again!! ... but I did learn the hard way, and, on one occasion in particular, I did discover the meaning of Grandma's words, and have since reflected on them with a certain respect.

Thankfully, my supping didn't bring me to the attention of the press, but as you read through the next few pages you will meet many people who did make the news, by courtesy of 'The Cup That Cheers'.

Cheers! Hic!   PHR

George Howforth, an agricultural labourer, was charged by Police Constable Suggitt with being drunk and disorderly at Cherry Burton on the 28th of January. About ten o'clock at night the defendant had stripped to fight, but was ordered off. A short time afterwards he was found propping himself against a wall, and, on the policeman coming up to him, he said he should make the officer find him a night's lodging. His demand was to some extent complied with, but finding that he was going to apartments furnished by the County he struck his conductor on the chest. Defence — 'Supped

freely and got fresh', fined 15s., including costs, or in default 21 days'
imprisonment.   FEBRUARY 1858
(*There's just no pleasing some folks.*)

John Smith, a Scotchman and Waterloo veteran, without pension or good-
conduct medal was brought up charged with being drunk and disorderly in
Lairgate at one o'clock on Christmas morning. Smith it appeared had been
under the command of Sir John Barleycorn, and while in active service
became so disabled in his limbs as to require the aid of a brick wall to keep
him anything like perpendicular. The strength of his lungs, however, more
than made up for the weakness of his limbs, as several persons in the
neighbourhood had ample proof in being aroused from their sweet repose.
Smith was taken prisoner by Sergeant Dunn who forthwith conveyed him
to the lock-up where he spent his Christmas. Fined 5s. for being drunk, and
allowed a week to pay it.   JANUARY 1859

Robert Danby and William Foster, publicans of Lund, were charged by
Police Constable Sanderson with keeping their houses open during divine
service on Sunday afternoon, the 1st *instant*. Sanderson deposed that about
a quarter to four o'clock in the afternoon he saw several persons in each
house with jugs and glasses before them. Danby, in defence, said that a
young man came from Cherry Burton to see a relative and he supplied him
with ale but was not aware that he had done wrong. He was now 76 years of
age and it was the first time in his life that any charge had been brought
against him. Foster admitted that some customers were in his house, but
there was more talking than drinking, and he did not draw a drop of beer
after 2 o'clock. As both the houses had been well conducted and the
defendants appearing to be ignorant of the law the cases were dismissed on
their paying the costs.   JANUARY 1860

Thomas Brown, labourer, was introduced by Constable Steel on a charge of
being drunk and incapable of taking care of himself the previous night,
having been found measuring his length upon the flagging between ten and
eleven o'clock. He was ordered to pay the usual drunkard's penalty, 5s.
(*Nowadays they appear able to remain upright longer.*)   MAY 1861

Thomas M'Dougal was charged with being drunk in Wilbert Lane at eleven
o'clock the previous night and using abusive language to Constables Bentley
and Clark. The accused, who had no defence to offer except that he was
lushy, was find 8s., including costs.   MARCH 1862
(*My dictionary defines lush as being fresh; juicy!*)

JANE DIXON, an old offender, who had a child with her about three years
of age, was charged with being drunk and creating a disturbance in Sweep
Row, *[at the Minster end of Keldgate]* at a late hour on Saturday night. She

was committed to prison for fourteen days and her child sent to the workhouse. MAY 1862

LOST TO DECENCY — William Robinson, bricklayer's labourer, was charged by P. C. Haldenby with being drunk on Saturday evening. The constable stated he found the defendant between six and seven o'clock lying in Playhouse Lane *[the northern section of Champney Road]* with his clothes disarranged. Several females had passed him whilst he was in that state. — Superintendent Knight said the defendant had been six times before the Bench since 1872. — The Mayor said it was a disgraceful case and he would be fined 40s. JUNE 1879

A LONG DRINKING BOUT — John Herring, hawker, was charged by Sergeant Tomlinson with being drunk and disorderly in the Market Place on the previous night. The Bench were informed that the prisoner had been drinking for three months. He was fined 5s. JULY 1881

(Continuously? Well, no wonder.)

ASSAULTS

Probably not what you may regard as entertaining or compulsive reading, but we have endeavoured to present a fair cross-section of these 'nasties', a few of which you will find are very reflective of today's society, and indicating that some things never change — Hence their inclusion. However, some are amusing — this again being through that wonderful style of reportage, and if you share our sense of humour we are sure you too will be amused at the interpretation of some of the wording.   PHR.

PHOTOGRAPHY.

J. GOULDING and CO., Artists and Photo-graphers, beg to announce that they have just brought out an entirely new kind of Portraiture for the Album (invented by themselves), consisting of three heads on one card, the centre one being in fine relief; and when artistically coloured, they are the neatest specimens of Carte-de-Visite ever yet introduced to the public.

Specimens may be seen and prices known, on application at their residence.

Butcher Row, Nov. 18th, 1865.

FIGHTING FOR A LEG OF PORK — William Giles was summoned by John Cole for assaulting him on Saturday night, the 19th December, under the following circumstances:— Cole lent Giles a shilling on the latter representing himself as being hard up and in want of a pint, although a previous loan to the same amount, and obtained under similar circumstances, was unliquidated. Cole afterwards bought a leg of pork for which Giles took a particular fancy and tried to get possession of it by frequently saying, 'I'll hook that leg of pork for you', which kind offers were declined with thanks. Failing in this he eventually knocked it out of his hand, and Cole was struck by Giles while endeavouring to regain it, the coveted joint being none the better from the accumulation of mud upon it

by rolling upon the ground. Giles' defence was that he was part owner of the pork, which was won at a raffle in which he went shares. Cole having sworn that it was a *bona fide* purchase, the defendant was fined 10s. including costs.   JANUARY 1864

BRUTAL ATTACK IN A PUBLIC STREET — On Thursday evening about half-past nine o'clock a most cowardly and disgraceful attack was made upon an elderly man named Button, a coachman in the service of Mrs. Hutton, Lair Gate. Mr. Button left the house of the latter immediately after prayers, and in turning into Landress Lane (where he resides) from Lair Gate was encountered by five young fellows, who asked him to give them a shilling. This he refused to do, whereupon they set about him, knocked him down, and caused blood to flow copiously from his head and face. Although stunned and injured by the blows he had received from the fall, he managed to reach his lodgings, which was only a few yards distant, and after washing himself he gave information to the police. The fact that this was near to the Central Street, and at no late hour, shows that the scamps were as impudent as they were cowardly, and, as the eye of suspicion is upon them, it is hoped that events may transpire which will lead to their detection.
                                                                   FEBRUARY 1866

NEIGHBOURS' DIFFERENCES — Alice Patterson was charged by Leonora Flear, her next-door neighbour, with assaulting her by throwing water upon her from her chamber window on Saturday morning. — Complainant stated that the defendant had swept the dirt on to the flags in front of her house and it was when going to the pump for some water to clean it off that the defendant threw the water upon her. She had not spoken to Mrs. Patterson for two months. — The defence was that Mrs. Flear had swept her dirt upon her flags. — The chairman said she had no right to go upstairs and throw water upon the complainant and she would have to pay a fine of 10s. There was evidently, he said, a good deal of ill-feeling between the parties, and if they came before the court again they would be bound over to keep the peace.   FEBRUARY 1878

(*Was the water really thrown from the chamber window, or could it have been that she threw the water from the chamber upon her from the window?*)

ASSAULTING A WIFE — George Clough, cow keeper, was charged before the Borough magistrates on Monday with assaulting his wife, and prayed he might be bound over to keep the peace. It appeared that when under the influence of drink defendant abused his wife, and he had been up several times previously. He was ordered to pay the costs and find bail for his good behaviour for six months or go to prison for a month.
                                                                     AUGUST 1886

(*No further comment!*)

ENTERTAINMENT

No cinema, radio or television — so what was available to entertain the townsfolk of Beverley? Well, there were, as you will have discovered if you have read our Alcohol section, plenty of public houses and inns, and there was, and still is, the Westwood should you fancy a walk or a ride — for those lucky enough to own a horse.

If drinking, walking or riding didn't appeal there were various halls of entertainment. Mr. Straker's wooden theatre in Hall Garth Field, sadly, no longer, and the old Assembly Rooms were, without doubt, a very popular venue for all kinds of shows and exhibitions, such as the 'interesting lecture' on Arab life; Boz the Wizard's 'exceedingly clever performance', and the 'extraordinary automatons' — Sam Baylis's Marionettes.

GRAND EXHIBITION OF BIRDS.

BEVERLEY ORNITHOLOGICAL SOCIETY.

Under the Patronage of the Mayor,
J. STEPHENSON, Esq., J.P.

THE Grandest Display of all kinds of BRITISH and FOREIGN BIRDS ever exhibited in Beverley,

IN THE

NEW CORN EXCHANGE,

ON WEDNESDAY, Nov. 24TH.

During the Exhibition there will be Music and Singing.

£40 *will be awarded in Prizes.*

Twenty-four valuable and useful Special Prizes kindly given by the Tradesmen of the town, which will be exhibited in the room.

Admission—From One to Three, 1s.; Two till close, 6d.

1436   R. DAWSON, HON. SEC.

Although not of this period, it's worth mentioning that the Assembly Rooms continued a fairly active role until 1935 when they were transformed into a more permanent hall of entertainment, the Regal Cinema, which was to continue as such until 1968, then bingo to date.

The Corn Exchange, built in 1886 and incorporating the Butter Market, had partitions which could be moved to form one large area, and was also used extensively for exhibitions, concerts and meetings, including the sketches and songs of a 'versatile gentleman' named Mr. Spurr. This was to continue until 1911 when the Corn Exchange became the Picture Playhouse, the town's first permanent picture hall, remaining as such today. (The full story can be found in 'The Home of Beautiful Pictures', our first book.

Read on and decide for yourselves if you could have managed in those days without your modern entertainments. PHR/RC

THE MAGIC ART — During the week, Professor Henri nightly entertained his audience with his cleverly performed illusions. By way of variation two vocalists, Madam Pattie Anderton and Mr. W. Wallace, sang several excellent songs in good style while Victoria, the Professor's daughter, in the capacity of clairvoyant did her part to perfection.
FEBRUARY 1865

THE PANTOMIMES — On Tuesday night last a late train from Hull to Beverley and Cottingham ran for the convenience of those desirous of witnessing the pantomimes at the theatres. That this act of courtesy on the part of the company was well appreciated is evinced by the great number who availed themselves of it Both the theatres on the occasion were crowded.
JANUARY 1866

Wombwell's Royal Menagerie (which, by the by, looks much less than it did formerly) visited Beverley on Thursday *en route* for Hull Fair. A number of other shows bound for the same fair also opened out, and the result was that for several hours in the evening the Market Place was all alive. Last night there was a similar display.
OCTOBER 1874

SAM BAYLIS'S MARIONETTES — Mr. Baylis with his extraordinary automatons has given performances in the Assembly Rooms during the past week to delighted audiences. We have both spoken of this exhibition, and therefore to go into detail would be but to recapitulate our praise. We may, however, remark, for the information of those whose misfortune it has been not to see the marionettes, that the entertainment is one of the most clever and extraordinary of the kind we have seen. The figures are life-like, the acting and gesticulations marvellous and the scenery and 'get up' splendid. There are two hours' good fun which few can spend without laughing

heartily. Mr. Baylis concludes this visit to Beverley to-night, so that there is yet a chance for those who have not seen his performance.

OCTOBER 1874

SKETCHES OF ARAB LIFE — Some of our readers will remember the interesting lecture given some time ago by Mustafa Ben Yusaf on Arab life and customs, which he illustrated by means of gentlemen who appeared in native costume. The same gentleman will deliver a discourse on the same subject in the Assembly Rooms next Tuesday evening when the Mayor will preside.

JUNE 1878

THE MOON — On Tuesday evening next, Mr. Ridway, F.R.A.S., will deliver a lecture on 'The Moon' with illustrations by oxyhydrogen light, in the Norwood School Room, in connection with the Church Institute.

MARCH 1879

(Oxyhydrogen light originates from a system comprised of a stream of oxygen blown through a flame of burning hydrogen producing a very hot flame, which, when played on a refractory substance, produces a light of great brilliance.)

BOZ, THE WIZARD — This talented conjurer gave an entertainment in the Assembly Rooms last night to an audience that were delighted with his exceedingly clever performance. A number of new tricks were introduced, and at the close he gave a dark seance, when he enacted the scenes which made the Davenport Brothers famous. By request he will give a children's performance at three this afternoon, and at eight in the evening appear in entirely new illusions. Boz is certainly worth a visit.

JANUARY 1880

29

NEW THEATRE — Mr. H. M. Straker has erected in the field near the Hall Garth Inn, a permanent theatre of wood. It is well fitted up, and will accommodate 600 or 700 persons. It was opened by a company last Monday evening, the play being, *All That Glitters Is Not Gold,* which was well put on the stage.   NOVEMBER 1881

(This entry is of particular interest from the point of the building's apparent size to accommodate that number of people. I feel it is sad that nothing remains today of this or other theatres in the town.)

NOVEL CRICKET MATCH — Next Tuesday a match is to be played on the recreation ground between the Dark Blues and Light Blues, colours which represent the Police and Butchers of Beverley respectively. Whether the Borough Police, who are accustomed to 'run 'em in' will in this instance run themselves out remains to be seen. The match is got up to help the Cottage Hospital.   JULY 1885

TREATS TO THE INMATES OF THE WORKHOUSE — On Thursday evening the inmates of the workhouse, numbering 131, were treated to a substantial knife and fork tea, through the kindness of Mr. and Mrs. Lycett Green, of Westwood. Mr. Frankish, the Market Place, was entrusted with the order of catering, and Mr. Dawe and his staff superintended the arrangements. The dining hall still retained its Christmas decorations, which added to the festivity. After the excellent tea the men and women were supplied with tobacco and tea and the children with oranges. Singing was indulged in, and a very pleasant evening, thanks to the donors, was spent.   JANUARY 1886

(We felt this Christmas treat worth including in this section as probably the knife and fork tea, tobacco and tea and singing brought a great amount of pleasure to the inmates.)

EAST RIDING ASYLUM — On Wednesday evening an entertainment was given to 150 of the patients of the Asylum by the Beverley handbell ringers, under the leadership of Mr. Davison. The entertainment, which consisted of songs, character sketches and pieces on the handbells, was well received and gave much pleasure to the audience.   FEBRUARY 1886

MIDSUMMER FAIR — This fair was held on Monday last, and like its predecessors of recent years it was a very tame affair. The show of horses and cattle was small and the pleasure part of the fair was reserved for the townspeople, countryfolk being conspicuous by their absence. The Market Place was pretty well filled with attractions of different kinds, shooting galleries, and stalls, and at night there was a throng for three or four hours.
                                                    JULY 1886

(One rather gets the impression the reporter didn't think much of the event.)

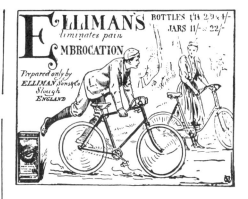
HEALTH AND BEAUTY

Our 'Health and Beauty' section offers no guarantees for any tips or cures you may wish to try or experiment with. But have you ever wanted to know a remedy for ringworm or chilblains? And I bet at some time or other you've had toothache or a sore throat. And how would you like to rid yourself of those unsightly freckles? Well, if there is anything that has already caught your attention, our 'Health and Beauty' section is for you. Over the next few pages we have entries on each of the above, plus a guide to help you live to 100 years — also why it's not healthy to lick stamps and envelopes. Do your hands perspire? Don't worry — you may find help inside. Whatever your interests in this section, please take notice at the end of one entry: 'Be governed by the advice of your physician.' Nevertheless, many old wives' tales may work — but who knows about old newspaper remedies ...?

PHR/RC

ANOTHER CURATIVE PROPERTY OF COD LIVER OIL — It has been recently discovered that this valuable medicine, in combination with chloroform in equal parts applied on lint, is an excellent alleviator of pain and an unfailing curative in scalds. This is really worth knowing, as most of us know the pain attendant on any accident of this description, and it is well to make known an effectual relief and cure.   JANUARY 1859

HAY FEVER — Surgeon Bradley says that, being tormented by one of the most distressing symptoms of hay-fever, incessant sneezing, and having tried all remedies suggested, in sheer desperation he plugged his nostrils with raw cotton. The effect was instantaneous — sneezing ceased. And, after repeatedly testing the remedy, he concludes that it is worth knowing and recommending.   MARCH 1883

CHILBLAINS — are very common with young people of delicate constitution and poor circulation. A good linament is the following: Oil of Turpentine, ¼ pint; Crushed Camphor, 1oz; Oil of Cajeput, 2 drachms; mix and agitate till the solution is complete. Rub the mixture on the unbroken surface two or three times daily.   FEBRUARY 1886

USEFUL PRECAUTION — A physician gives the following useful hints on health: Never lean the back on anything that is cold. Never begin a journey until the breakfast has been eaten. Never take warm drinks and then immediately go out in the cold air. Keep the back, especially between the shoulderblades, well covered; also the chest well protected. Never go to bed with cold, damp feet; always toast them before a fire for 10 or 15 minutes before retiring. When hoarse, speak as little as possible until you are recovered, else the voice may be permanently lost or difficulties of the throat may be produced. Merely warm the back by the fire and never continue keeping the back exposed to this heat after it has become comfortably warm. To do otherwise is debilitating. When going from a warm atmosphere into a colder one keep the mouth closed, so that the air may be warmed by its passage through the nose ere it reaches the lungs. Never stand still in cold weather, especially after having taken a slight degree of exercise; and always avoid standing upon the ice or snow, or where the person is exposed to a cold wind.   FEBRUARY 1886

LONGEVITY — In order to live a hundred years it has been announced that you must breathe all the out-of-door air possible, and breathe it deeply, and that you must take your sleep as nature indicates, 8 or 9 hours in the early part of the dark, which will allow you to be up fully refreshed at sunrise. In addition to these important items of sleep and breath, it is further declared that you must not permit yourself to get angry or to fret and worry; but that, if you must, at once take a bath and some immediate slumber; that you must eat more vegetables and grains and fruit and meats, and dismiss wines and spirits, coffee and tea; that you must bathe often, wear loose clothing, and keep warm; and that you must control your appetites and passions, cultivate cheerful serenity, and be governed by the advice of your physician.   MAY 1886

(Definitely worth taking note of.)

HEALTHY ALPHABET — The Ladies Sanitary Association of London gives the following simple rules for keeping health.
A-s soon as you are up, shake blanket and sheet;
B-etter be without shoes than sit with wet feet;
C-hildren, if healthy, are active, not still;
D-amp beds and damp clothes will both make you ill;
E-at slowly and always chew your food well;
F-reshen the air in the house where you dwell;

G-arments must never be made too tight;
H-omes should be healthy, airy and light;
I-f you wish to be well, as you do have no doubt,
J-ust open the windows before you go out;
K-eep the rooms always tidy and clean;
L-et the dust on the furniture never be seen;
M-uch illness is caused by the want of pure air;
N-ow, to open the windows be ever your care;
O-ld rags and old rubbish should never be kept;
P-eople should see that their floors are well swept;
Q-uick movements in children are healthy and right;
R-emember the young cannot thrive without light;
S-ee that the cistern is clean to the brim;
T-ake care that your dress is all tidy and trim;
U-se your nose to find if there be a bad drain;
V-ery sad are the fevers that come in its train;
W-alk as much as you can without fear and fatigue;
X-erxes could walk full many a league;
Y-our health is your wealth, which your wisdom must keep;
Z-eal will help a cause, and the goods you will keep.

MAY 1886

MISTAKES — It is a mistake to labour when you are not in a fit condition to do so;

To think that the more a person eats the healthier and stronger he will become;

To go to bed at midnight and rise at daybreak, and imagine that every hour taken from sleep is an hour gained;

To imagine if a little work or exercise is good, violent or prolonged exercise is better;

To conclude the smallest room in the house is large enough to sleep in;

To eat as if you had only a minute to finish the meal in, or to eat without an appetite, or to continue after it has been satisfied merely to please the taste;

To believe that children can do as much work as grown people, and that the more hours they study the more they learn;

To imagine that whatever remedy causes one to feel immediately better (as alcohol stimulates) is good for the system, without regard to the after effects;

To take off proper clothing out of season because you have become heated;

To sleep exposed to direct draught;

To think any nostrum or patent medicine is a specific for all the diseases flesh is heir to.   JUNE 1886

(What's that? The smallest room — large enough to sleep in? Not ours.)

CHECKED PERSPIRATION — Is the fruitful cause of sickness, disease, and death to multitudes every year. Heat is constantly generated within the human body by the chemical disorganisation, the combustion of the food we eat. There are several millions of tubes or pores on the surface of the body, which in health are constantly open. If they are closed, two things take place. First, the internal heat which has answered its purpose is prevented from passing off, to accumulate every moment. A person expresses himself as burning up, and large draughts of water are swallowed to quench the internal fire — This we call 'fever'. But another result follows the closing of the pores in the skin, and is more immediately dangerous; a main outlet of the waste of the body is closed, it re-mingles with the blood, which in a few hours becomes impure, and begins to generate disease in every fibre of the system. — The whole machinery of the man becomes at once disordered, and he expresses himself as 'feeling miserable'.

The terrible effects of checked perspiration of a dog, who sweats only by his tongue, is evinced by his becoming 'mad'. The water runs in streams from a dog's mouth in summer if exercising it freely. If it ceases to run that is 'hydrophobia'. It has been asserted by a French physician that if a person suffering under 'hydrophobia' can be only made to perspire freely he is cured at once. It is familiar to the commonest observer that in all ordinary forms of disease the patient begins to get better the moment he begins to perspire, simply because the internal heat is passing off, and there is an outlet for the waste of the system. — (*The Family Doctor*)   JUNE 1886

(*If this became common knowledge the anti-perspirant market would collapse overnight — and in no time at all we could become healthier but smelly!*)

POWDERED RICE is said to have a great effect in stopping bleeding from flesh wounds.   JUNE 1886

(*I'd rather use Elastoplast.*)

TOOTHACHE — For ordinary nervous toothache, which is caused by the nervous system being out of order or by excessive fatigue, a very hot bath will be found an excellent remedy. This will so soothe the nerves that sleep will naturally follow, and upon getting up the patient will feel much refreshed and the toothache will be a thing of the past. For what is known as 'jumping' toothache, a hot dry flannel applied to the face and neck is very effective. For common toothache caused by indigestion or by strong sweet acid, or anything hot or cold in a decayed tooth, a little piece of cotton steeped in a camphorated spirit or oil of cloves is the best remedy.

(Or seek advice from a painless dentist) JUNE 1886

SUNSTROKE — When one is attacked by sunstroke a doctor should be sent for at once. Until he arrives the patient should be carried to a cool and shaded place, all tight garments loosened, and cold water wrung from a cloth applied to the head. He should be fanned. It's so serious is the attack and its effects, that what is of most importance for the public to know are its causes, and how to prevent it. Soldiers, especially, and those most exposed, as in harvest work &c., are very liable to sunstroke. Weakness and ill health predispose to an attack. All tight and heavy clothing should be avoided — water should be taken freely as required, but not in excess, and certainly not immediately after violent exercise, when one is overheated and perspiring freely. Nobody should go into the sunshine bareheaded, the inside of the crown of the hat might be lightly filled with white muslin, or a fresh cabbage leaf may be inserted. The back of the head should be screened by something fresh, light and porous. The value of such simple details, punctually carried out as habits, cannot be overrated. JULY 1886

THE CORSET HABIT — Miss Fullard writes: 'When women now old tell me of the brass stomachers and terrific high heels worn by their grandmothers, and that in their own youths they strung their corsets by making a fulcrum of the bedpost and pulling with all their might and main, I breathe freer metaphorically speaking and think some women at least are coming to their senses, and keep urging the introduction of hygiene as a special study in all branches of public schools. We need this as women hardly less than do our brothers; for I verily believe, and shamefacedly confess, that the corset habit among women is as difficult to break as the alcohol and tobacco habit among men. If the Laws of God that seek the health of the body were obeyed by but a single generation, the next one would be physically beautiful.' JULY 1886

(Should you not wish to break the 'habit', then see our ad for Mrs. Wynn, Corset Maker, Vicar Lane — March 1880)

WARM BATHS — Will often prevent the most virulent diseases. A person who may be in fear of having received infection of any kind should take a warm bath, suffer perspiration to ensure, and then rub dry. Dress warmly to guard against taking cold. If the system has imbibed any infectious matter, it will be removed by resorting to this process; if done before the infection has had time to spread over the system, and, even if some time has elapsed, the drenching perspiration that may be induced by hot water will be very certain to remove it.   JULY 1886

(Marvellous what a warm bath can do for you, isn't it?)

RINGWORMS, it is said, can be cured in 10 days by cutting the hair of the affected part, rubbing in turpentine and washing off with carbolated soap. Then wash the whole head with hot water and touch the spots with dilute tincture of iodine, repeating once or twice a day.   JULY 1886

SIMPLE CURE FOR SORE THROAT — Everyone has a cure for sore throats, but simple remedies appear to be most effectual. Salt and water is used by many as a gargle, but a little alum and honey dissolved in sage tea is better. An application of cloths wrung out in hot water and applied to the neck, changing as often as they begin to feel cool, has the most potency for removing inflammations of anything we ever tried. During the evening is usually the most convenient time for applying this remedy.   JULY 1886

FEMALE BEAUTY — There is nothing more unfavourable to female beauty than late hours. Women who spend most of the day in bed and the night at work or dissipation have always a pale, faded complexion and dark rimmed, wearied eyes. Too much sleep is almost as hurtful as too little and is sure to bloat the person with a pallid and unwholesome fat. A gross and excessive indulgence in eating and drinking is fatal to the female charms. The appetite should never be wasted during the intervals between meals on pastry, confectionery, or any other tickler of the appetite which gratifies the taste but does not support the system. Exercise is, of course, essential to female beauty.   JULY 1886

NEURALGIA — One of the best remedies for neuralgia is quinine. In all cases in which there is any suspicion of ague or when the patient is residing in a district where ague is prevalent, this is the remedy to give. It is indicated too when the attacks come on at regular intervals. It has long been recognised that quinine readily controls that form of neuralgia in which pain is experienced at the point just above one or other of the eyebrows. Quinine to do any good in neuralgia must be taken in fairly large doses. Thus two tablespoonfuls of strong quinine mixture should be taken every four hours. Some chemists now keep 5 grain quinine pills made up with a drop or two of syrup; and by many these will be preferred to the mixture. One should be

taken very four hours. Quinine is said to control neuralgia and ordinary face ache more effectively when the powder is taken in small quantities every few minutes — as much, for instance, as will adhere to the tip of the finger dipped into the powder. We need hardly point out the importance of getting your quinine pure. The three great indications for the use of quinine are — (1) Suspicion of ague; (2) Paroxysms being periodical; (3) Pain being experienced chiefly over eyebrow. Very obstinate cases of neuralgia, which have resisted all other treatment. The Germans often give what we should consider enormous doses of quinine — from 40 grains to two drachms a day. — *The Family Physician.* JULY 1886
(According to the dictionary ague is intermittent malarial fever, marked by fits of shivering, burning, sweating.)

LICKING STAMPS AND ENVELOPES — This is a perilous practice against which the public needs to be put on its guard. We have seen bad consequences ensue from the habit which is a very bad one. Those who are frequently thus moistening the gum on adhesive surfaces suffer from local irritation, sore tongues and the like, while every now and again we hear a special remonstration on the way in which diseases may be communicated. One such was recently brought under our notice. An envelope received from a person who habitually took large quantities of morphia hypodermically was re-closed by the person who opened it by licking the adhesive surface, with the result of making him violently sick. The mere touch of his tongue of the taker of morphia had rendered the gum intensely nauseous. If this could happen obviously there must be grave peril of the transmission of disease by such means. It is not likely that many persons would ever intentionally re-close an envelope in this way; but the incident may serve to show how desirable it is not to run the risk of ever taking in the impurities of new adhesive matters. It is very easy to avoid the practice. The danger only needs to be pointed out. — *The Lancet.* JULY 1886

FRECKLES — Powered nitre moistened with water applied to the face night and morning will soon remove all traces of freckles. AUGUST 1886

HICCOUGHS in nine cases out of ten can be stopped by an effort of the will or by simply holding the breath. Sudden fright almost invariably stops it. AUGUST 1886

38

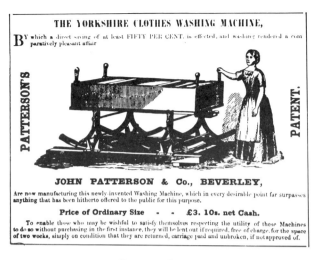
HOME CARE

Speaking confidentially, the girl can't overhear us, can she? No, she can't — that's good. Are you having any trouble with your servant? How often do you reprimand, or have reprimanded, her for her lack of consideration when putting coals on the fire? Do you find she just throws them on with little regard for that sick relative, the poorly thing who jumps and shudders each time the girl 'mends' the fire, and your inability to find a solution or a quieter girl? It's just possible your worries will soon be over, for help is near. Within our 'Home Care' pages we have included a complete guide for everything your servant should know about putting coals on the fire silently! We would, however, respectfully suggest that you do not allow your servant to have access to your copy of this book, but allow yourself the

extravagence of a treat (from her own wages) and get her a copy, for not only will she learn to care for the fire properly, but could also benefit from many other entries, all to your advantage. (May we respectfully suggest to Madam that you ensure your servant can read: otherwise you may just find this book propping up that short table leg.)

Without hesitation we do highly recommend 'Home Care' to Madam. We are confident you won't regret a single penny spent. It's a small price to pay for the high return from your girl. **PHR**

OUR BOYS — Boys are often considered little more than animate depravity. But give them a chance. Put a boy upon his honour, trust him, and he will be trusty. It is the boy, and girl, too, for that matter, who is always suspected of doing wrong who does it. Show them that they are not unmitigated nuisances, and do not send them out into the street to learn wickedness, with the idea that, 'Mama doesn't care', if they are only out of her sight and hearing. Give them also good books without the adventure and profanity and brutality of the greater part of the present stories for boys, boys having, at best, sufficient of the savage instinct without a special literature to cultivate it. **APRIL 1882**

WHICH IS THE WEAKER SEX? — Females are called the weaker sex, but why? If they are not strong, who is? When men must wrap themselves in thick garments and encase the whole in a stout overcoat to shut out the cold, women in thin silk dresses, with neck and shoulders bare, or nearly so, say they are perfectly comfortable! When men wear waterproof boots over woollen hose, and encase the whole in india rubber to keep them from freezing, women wear thin silk hose and cloth shoes and pretend not to feel the cold! When men cover their heads with furs, and then complain of the severity of the weather, women hang an apology for a bonnet at the back of their heads, and ride or walk about in north east winds, professing not to suffer at all! **JANUARY 1884**
(There could be something in that. Even today our women dress in a lot less than men!)

Whole cloves are now used to exterminate the merciless and industrious moth. It is said they are more effectual as a destroying agent than either tobacco, camphor or cedar shavings. **SEPTEMBER 1885**
(Hadn't moth balls been invented?)

Husbands should make confidants of their wives, consulting them on their plans and prospects, and especially on their troubles and embarrassments. A woman's intuition is often better than all the shrewdness and wisdom of a man; and all her ready sympathy and interest is a powerful aid to his efforts for their mutual welfare. JANUARY 1886
This male chauvinist pig suspects this was written by a woman.)

Powdered cinnamon will scatter black and red ants effectually. Let it be strewn in backs of cupboard shelves, and along the edges of tin cake boxes, and the pests will soon disappear. This, with red pepper (cayenne), will be sufficient to remove them, however firmly they may seem to be established. JANUARY 1886

Home sweet Home! — The sweetest houses in this town are those where Hudson's extract of soap is in daily use. JANUARY 1886

To remove a tight ring — Wind a piece of cotton twine well soaked as tightly as possible around the finger, commencing at the tip and winding until the ring is reached, press the end under the ring with the head of a needle and unwind. The ring will come off with it. FEBRUARY 1886

Putting Coals on the Fire — The sick and those who watch by their bedsides know how terribly disturbing is the noise of 'putting coals' on the fire, whether they be violently thrown on in the manner generally adopted by servants and nurses (skilled or otherwise), or placed more carefully with the tongs, as kind relatives or friends will sometimes 'make-up the fire' in their sympathy with the sufferer! Even under the most careful manipulation loose pieces of coal are almost sure to fall, and the disturbing rattle is the result. This may appear to be a very small matter to look back upon, but at the time it is by no means unimportant, and in some cases very great distress and even injury may be produced by it. A very simple precaution will suffice to prevent the annoyance altogether. If a few paper bags be supplied to the servant who replenishes the coal box, and these are filled with pieces of coal, nothing can be easier than to lift one or more of these packages onto the fire noiselessly and so settle them that, when the paper burns, the coals may not fall out of the grate. By this obvious method a noiseless coal fire may be secured. FEBRUARY 1886
(This is one of our favourites.)

If you wish to prevent the unpleasant odour that arises from boiling cabbage tie up a piece of stale bread in a muslin cloth and boil with the cabbage. A piece of stale bread on the end of a knife with which you cut onions will prevent the juice from affecting the eyes unpleasantly. MARCH 1886

PAPER PILLOW — Save all the scraps of writing paper, old envelopes *etc.*, cut them into strips about ½ inch wide, and 2 inches long and curl them well with an old pen knife. Make a pillow case of any material you have, fill it with your curled paper mixed with a few shreds of flannel. Stuff it quite full, sew the end up and cover it as you please. These pillows are invaluable in cases of fever as they keep continually cool.   APRIL 1886

CARE OF CLOTHES — Very nice dresses which are only worn occasionally should be folded up and carefully pinned up in tissue paper, put in boxes or drawers, to exclude dust and air; while dresses in everyday wear are best hung up in closets. Always brush your bonnet or hat when you take it off your head; it will last much longer if the dust is removed in this way, and will always be ready to put on. Gloves should have the fingers pulled out lengthways, and laid one on the other, silk gloves the same, and all kept in a proper box. Have a box or cupboard shelf in a closet appropriated to shoes, and make a point of keeping them there; if left standing about the room or under beds they get dusty and become shabby much sooner than they ought. Veils, ties, ribbons, belts should all be carefully folded as soon as taken off the person. Nightclothes should be hung up to air during the day and not placed under the pillow.   MAY 1886

(Definitely useful advice for those expensive designer clothes.)

THINGS A HOUSEKEEPER SHOULD KNOW

That salt should be eaten with nuts to aid digestion.
That milk which stands too long makes bitter butter.
That rusty flat irons should be rubbed over with beeswax and lard.
That it rests you in sewing to change your position frequently.
That a hot strong lemonade taken at bedtime will break up a bad cold.
That tough meat is made tender by lying a few minutes in vinegar and water.
That a little soda water will relieve a sick headache caused by indigestion.
That a cup of strong coffee will remove the odour of onions from the breath.
That a cup of hot water drunk before meals will prevent nausea and dyspepsia.
That well-ventilated bedrooms will prevent morning headaches and lassitude.
That one in a faint should be laid flat on his back; then loosen his clothes and let him alone.
That consumptive night sweats may be arrested by sponging the body nightly in salt water.
That a fever patient can be made cool and comfortable by frequently sponging off with soda water.
That to beat the whites of eggs quickly, add a pinch of salt. Salt cools, and cold eggs froth rapidly.
That the hair may be kept from falling out after illness by a frequent application to the scalp of sage tea.
That you can take out spots from washed goods by rubbing them with the yolk of eggs before washing.

That white spots upon varnished furniture will disappear if you hold a hot plate over them.   MAY 1886

(After reading that I bet you are now left wondering how you ever managed without knowing about them.)

To keep lamps from smoking dip the wick in strong, hot vinegar. Dry it before putting it in the lamp.   JUNE 1886

SOME DON'TS FOR LADIES

Don't disturb your husband while he is reading his evening paper by asking him foolish questions. He may be only reading the latest scandal, but he is just as much interested as though it were foreign news or market reports. Be patient and when he comes across anything he thinks you can comprehend perhaps he may read it to you. Don't communicate unpleasant news or ask a favour before eating. The heart is not easily touched when the stomach is empty. Don't be unreasonably vexed if he is not ready for church as soon as you are. If he doesn't start to get ready until the bells begin to ring, you mustn't expect the same result as with yourself, who had the whole morning before you go. Don't scold him because he leaves the ashes in his pipe. One of the privileges of a married man is to leave an old pipe full of ashes in just the position to empty the contents onto the window sill, or the mantelpiece the moment it is touched. Don't *parlez* the last word in a discussion. The sooner you discover that it is a pleasure you must forgo, and make up your mind to relinquish it entirely, the sooner you have a chance for peace in the family, and a longer life of fireside contentment.   JULY 1886

(Home Sweet Home)

HOW TO GET RID OF RATS

To those who suffer the depradations of rats and whose consciences will permit of their descending to any depths of meanness and duplicity in order to rid themselves of their pests, the following suggestions may prove useful; attempts to catch rats by traps or by poisoning them suddenly will fail. Old rats know too much and can only be caught by kindness. To destroy them, give them a good meal every day. Do not put any poison in the food; but simply prepare for them a dish daily, as a free lunch, composed of cornmeal moistened with milk into which egg and a little salt (to season) has been beaten. At first they may not touch it; keep it before them, making it fresh daily. They will soon try a little, and, if not injurious, their suspicions will be allayed. In a week or ten days they will expect it, and every rat will be at the appointed place for the treat. Give them plenty of it, so as to induce all the rats from the neighbourhood to join in. Do not be in a hurry to poison them. If they eat all the food give them a larger quantity next time. As soon as they have thrown off all suspicion, go to your druggist, get some phosphorous paste, or other rat poison, mix it with the food, and be sure you give them enough and some to spare, so as to induce all to eat. They will either be killed or become so suspicious of all other food as to leave, and not a rat will remain. Hence, to destroy rats take plenty of time, gain their confidence and finish them when they least expect it.   AUGUST 1886

MISCELLANEOUS LOCAL INTEREST

We feel this is probably the most fascinating section of the book. This was the place we 'stuck' everything we couldn't find a home for. In no time at all we had collected a great wealth of local bits too numerous to categorize. Some of the little gems included are the sad report of the boy sent up the chimney to clean it and a full coverage of a wonderful and memorable trip to Hornsea. Read about the 'stink' created by the poor unfortunates who found the easy way into Hell Garth sewer. Permit us to introduce you to 'a nice young man' named Samuel Fountain, who made improper advances to an 'ancient looking dame'. Also, we have included what may easily be the first local offence reported of a graffiti artist at work. PHR/PAH

John Green, agricultural servant to Mr. Robert Fisher, of Leckonfield, *(sic)* was charged by his master with refusing to obey his orders and general disorderly conduct, which defendant did not deny.
Ordered to go back and fulfil contract, and wages to be reduced by £1.
FEBRUARY 1856

John Roberts, a fellow with one leg, was charged by Mr. Wilkinson, of the Buck Inn, Beckside, with creating a disturbance in his house, and breaking 16 out of 20 panes of glass in his window on Saturday night last. Committed for 21 days' hard labour. SEPTEMBER 1856

BEVERLEY CATTLE MARKET: FEB. 25 — A good supply of beasts, and a fair supply of sheep. A good attendance of customers, and all stock changed hands. Beef 7s. to 7s.6d. per stone; mutton 8d. to 8½d. per pound.

(What price per pound per customer?)
FEBRUARY 1857

John Johnson, a chimney sweep, was summoned, on the information of John Groves, for allowing a boy about 13 years of age to ascend a chimney, on the 13th *instant*. Wilberforce Herdsman, in whose house the affair took place, appeared for defendant, and stated that he (Herdsman) had engaged the boy to sweep the chimney, which could not be swept properly by any other means. Fined £5, or seven days' imprisonment, and Herdsman was informed that he had rendered himself liable to a similar penalty had the information been laid against him. OCTOBER 1857

SCHOOL TRIP TO HORNSEA — On Monday last about 350 boys and girls belonging to the Minster schools were conveyed to the above delightful spot in sixteen waggons, which had been kindly lent for the occasion by several farmers in the parish of St. John. The procession through Hornsea to the sea-side, headed by the Temperance band, had a very pleasing appearance. The juveniles were accompanied by the Rev. J. B. Birtwhistle, Rev. G. Swift, and Mr. L. Robinson. During the day the rising generation were bountifully supplied with buns and milk, which seemed to be greatly enjoyed. There was only one mishap, and that of no very serious nature, which was that a boy had become so interested in seeing a man catching shrimps that he by accident was left behind but fortunately was taken care of by an uncle and brought home the next day by his parents, who made a journey on purpose to do so. JULY 1858

William Wilson, William Hardy, George Shaw, John Boynton, and Charles Pinder were summoned for obstructing a footpath in Bishop Burton on the night of Sunday 30th of October, and by their cursing, swearing, whistling, shouting, and other misconduct, the congregation in the Wesleyan Chapel was greatly disturbed. The case not being proved against Pinder, he was discharged, but the others were bound over in £10 to keep the peace for six months, and to pay the costs. NOVEMBER 1859

FATAL TERMINATION OF A MARRIAGE — William Lawson, farm servant, who was married about ten days ago in this town, on returning from the church, was seized with lockjaw and spasms, never spoke afterwards and died in the course of six days. It is supposed to have been brought on from having slept in a damp bed. He had the attendance of four medical men, but it proved of no avail. MAY 1860

Patrick Conniff, an Irishman, was charged with running through the streets almost in a state of nudity. It appearing that the defendant was subject to insanity, he was dismissed. JULY 1860

(Just think: nowadays it would be called streaking.)

Mary Tasker, a girl, appeared before the court at the instance of the Mayor, for wheeling a barrow along the flagging in Walkergate. His Worship said that his object in ordering her to attend instead of being summoned was to warn her and others that offences of this description subjected the delinquents to a penalty of forty shillings, which fine would in future be enforced on all who were convicted as the practice had become very common. She was then discharged. OCTOBER 1860

(Almost fined forty shillings, called a delinquent and just for wheeling her barrow on the pavement!)

FISHWICK'S MILL BURNT DOWN — On Monday night last, 2nd Sept., the inhabitants of this town were thrown into great excitement consequent upon the wilful and malicious destruction of the house and premises belonging to the corporation, and which had been occupied by the Messrs. Fishwick and their ancestors for a great number of years. The tenants gave up possession of the premises a few days since, having previously taken down the mill, but leaving materials to the value of £20. The outrage, which was loudly condemned by a vast majority of the freemen of the town, will prove a lasting disgrace to the perpetrators, that of wantonly destroying the dwelling house, for which about 25 or 30 of them will, we understand, have to answer at the York Assizes. The men broke into the dwelling and destruction then began in earnest. All panes of glass were broken, window frames knocked out, the boards riven up and the doors and shutters riven off their hinges. Tiles were thrown off the roof and damage was also done to the garden and hedge. The house and premises were eventually set alight at 8 o'clock, according to rumour by straw placed under the staircase and set alight. By Tuesday morning the premises were reduced to a charred shell. The council intend to prosecute the misguided offenders at the York Assizes. SEPTEMBER 1861

(The mill was, in the opinion of the freemen, built on common pasture and therefore accessible to them. Their fury had been invigorated by the council regarding anyone found on the premises as a trespasser.)

TURNER'S CHARITY — The first distribution of the above charity in sums of £10.10s. each, to well conducted, honest, deserving, sober and discreet domestic servants, pursuant to the will of the late Matthew

Turner, Esq., took place in the Norwood Assembly Rooms, Thursday last. The Mayor (James Mowld Robinson, Esq.), presided, and in the presence of the other trustees, the Rev. B. Brander, the Rev. J. B. Birtwhistle, and Mr. F. Denton, distributed the above munificent sums to the successful candidates, after a brief but appropriate address in which he trusted that the fortunate recipients would maintain that excellent character they had borne, and the unsuccessful candidates would not be dispirited but persevere, and they would in future overcome their difficulties. There were no less than 240 applicants, a fact which was highly creditable to Beverley and the neighbourhood. The names of the successful candidates, 68 in number, were read over.   FEBRUARY 1862

TREAT TO WORKMEN — On Wednesday evening the workmen employed by Mr. M. L. Whitton, builder, numbering about 30, sat down to an excellent supper given by their employer and provided by Mr. Holmes of the Rose and Crown Inn. — Mr. C. Arnott, cabinet maker, North Bar Street, also gave his annual treat of roast beef and plum pudding to his workmen the same evening, which was provided by Mr. W. Boyes, of the Kings Arms Inn. — On Christmas Eve, Mr. J. B. Lowther, coal merchant, Beckside, according to his annual custom, gave about 8lbs. of beef to each of his workmen.   JANUARY 1863

(It goes to prove there was some good in those old days.)

Celebrations for the marriage between His Royal Highness The Prince of Wales to The Princess Alexandra of Denmark, on March 10 1863, were not just confined to London, for here in Beverley the occasion was marked in grand style as the Beverley Guardian *reported on Saturday, March 14 and 21, as will be seen from the extracts that follow:*

On Monday afternoon flags were suspended from several windows, the first, we believe, being two handsome ones suspended from a line extending across the street from the shop of Messrs. T. and G. Swailes, nursery and seedman, in Toll Gavel to that of Mrs. Hardwick, butcher on the opposite side.

The Procession: This was appointed to take place at eleven o'clock at which time, in a heavy snow storm, the members of the Odd Fellows' Society arrived and took up their position in Toll Gavel, as previously arranged. The Foresters also appeared in Cross Street, and a start was then made. The bands, as they passed through the streets, played alternately *The National Anthem, Rule Britannia,* and *The British Grenadiers.*

The Dinners, *&c:* The first in order was the one given to the poor men and women of sixty years of age and upwards in the Hall of the Mechanics Institute. At half-past five in the afternoon between sixty and seventy gentleman sat down to a dinner at the Beverley Arms most admirably provided by Mr. Morley, whose cuisine it is quite superfluous to say anything in praise of.

The Illuminations: We now proceed to give some description of the

48

above, which was upon a most magnificent scale, commencing with the North Bar. On both sides in gas jets were displayed the letters A.E. and A.C., the two letters combined, a brilliant star forming the centre. The pillar in the centre of Wednesday Market bore a brilliant star, composed of gas jets, together with a wreath twisted round the column.

The fireworks, although of a first-class character, were not so extensive as many were led to imagine, considering the large sum devoted to that purpose.

CELEBRATION COMMITTEE — At a meeting of the above committee held yesterday the following statement of accounts was presented:— Amount of subscriptions, £258.13s.9d. Disbursements — For fireworks, £60.9s; Dinner to the aged poor, £43.7s.1d; Balls, £20.10s.6d; Tea, *etc.*, For the children, £78; Bands, banners *etc.*, £28.1s; Printing and advertising, £18.14s; Incidental expenses, £9.12s; Total, £258.13s.7d.

We have been informed by the Post Master that upwards of 1500 copies of the *Beverley Guardian*, of Saturday last, containing a report of the rejoicings in this town and neighbourhood passed through the Post Office on Sunday, Monday and Tuesday. MARCH 1863

A NASTY DIP — John Taylor of Beckside was brought up by P.C. Fidler, charged with being drunk and incapable the day previous. Taylor, it seems, got so intoxicated that he fell into the open sewer that runs along Hell Garth Lane from which he was dragged out in a condition better imagined than described, and, being thickly coated with slime and filth, his father would not own him; consequently he had to be taken to the lock-up to be purified. He was fined 5s. or in default to be committed to prison for seven days. APRIL 1863
(Apparently the sewer in Hell Garth Lane was noted for being one of the 'best' of its type as far as any sewer goes!)

CHRISTMAS TREAT — The usual Christmas treat was given to the inmates of the workhouse, and consisted of roast beef, plum pudding, *etc.*, the men being afterwards regaled with tobacco, the women with tea, and the children with oranges, nuts and raisins. JANUARY 1864

A NICE YOUNG MAN — Samuel Fountain, 20 years of age, farm servant to Mr. John Seamer of Arram, was brought up by warrant to answer a charge of misconduct of a very singular character. Very early on Monday morning last, Mrs. Seamer, an ancient looking dame, rather frosted with age, having seen several winters, was in bed by herself enjoying a comfortable snooze, her worthy lord and master having been called away on business, when the aforesaid Samuel appeared unto her, not in a dream, but attired in white. While holding a lighted candle over the astonished dame he with more boldness than delicacy popped the question as to whether she would have him as a bedfellow, to which she indignantly replied, 'No, I sure I sha'n't,' and then added, in unmistakable terms, 'If I had a good knobbed stick, I would crack your skull for you, that I would.' In the course of her evidence which she gave with her back turned towards the defendant she reminded the court that she '*did*' scold him, and also intimated that she heard him on the stairs twice before he came into her room, but his heart failed him. She ordered him out of the house, but at night when her husband came home a policeman was sent for and she had him 'ta'en up' for his conduct towards her. All that Fountain said in defence was that he was sorry, and did not know what he was doing. The contract was dissolved and the defendant's wages deducted, he being ordered to pay the costs.

FEBRUARY 1864

(I wonder how the 'ancient looking dame' felt at her description by the press — a bit unkind after what she went through.)

SEVERE THUNDER STORM — During the storm which passed over this town yesterday afternoon a house in Henfield belonging to Mrs. Hayes was greatly injured, as the lightning penetrated the roof, tore the plastering from the ceiling and walls, and then passed through a pane of glass in the window.

MAY 1864

OPENING OF THE BEVERLEY AND MARKET WEIGHTON RAILWAY — On Monday last the above line was opened without any ceremonial. The first train leaving Hull for York, *via* Market Weighton, at 6.40 a.m.; and one in the opposite direction at 7.10 a.m. The trains, on their arrival at the stations between Beverley and Market Weighton, were received by the wondering inhabitants of the district with admiration, the boys doing their full share in honour of the event by heartily cheering. On the occasion of the opening of the above line, Mr. Jackson, the contractor, gave a substantial dinner of roast beef and plum pudding to about 200 of his workmen, which was provided by Mr. Simpson of the Londesbro' Arms Hotel, Market Weighton, in first class style and was served up in a large building, kindly lent for the occasion by T. W. Rivis, Esq. It should be added that the navvies behaved themselves in a most respectful manner, not even a wrong word being heard amongst them.   MAY 1865

A WANDERER — Thomas Martin, a boy, 13 years of age, was brought up by P.C. Anderson, who found him in Fleming Gate at two o'clock that morning in a destitute condition. He was detained till his friends were communicated with.   MAY 1865

PEDESTRIANISM — On Monday evening a large crowd was drawn together on the York Road, through the medium of the bellman, to see a man named Thompson walk a distance of two miles against time. The feat was accomplished in 18 minutes, after which the pedestrian's daughter, a little girl four years of age, neatly attired in white, ran, according to announcement, 100 yards in 30 seconds. On Tuesday evening a similar exhibition took place when the distances were increased, the man walking three miles in 27 minutes, and the child running 200 yards in 60 seconds. Thompson, who is a stranger, was accompanied by a woman, who looked after the needful by going round with the hat during the performances, and in this respect the results were very satisfactory.   SEPTEMBER 1865

THE WEATHER — The past week, unlike its predecessor, has been characterised by weather more like winter than spring time. Intensely cold northerly and easterly winds, accompanied by severe frosts at nights, have been the prevailing elements, and vegetation has been very much kept back. May Day was remarkable for snow and hail storms.   MAY 1866
(Some things don't appear to change much, do they?)

FOULING A WELL — George Stephenson, a respectable looking lad, was summoned for having rendered foul a well in the town street of Cherry Burton by kicking into it a dead rat on Friday, the 29th *ult.* Defendant pleaded that it had been done unintentionally and that he was sorry for what had taken place. It transpired that his mother had spent nearly the whole of the night trying to get the animal out again. Dismissed with a caution on payment of costs. JULY 1866

(At least he was a respectable looking lad, but what about his poor mother? I admire her.)

A FREAK — On Monday night some of the inmates of the Militia Barracks were surprised to see a woman, somewhat poorly clad, deliberately begin to undress herself in front of the building. She was remonstrated with, and, after a short conversation, she walked into the house of one of the sergeants and coolly took off her bonnet and shawl, preparing herself, to the surprise of the inmates, for a stay for the night. The incoherent and rambling manner in which she answered the questions put to her soon led to the discovery that she was *non compos mentis* and the police were sent for, who took her into custody. On the following day Supt. Hopkinson discovered that she had walked from Hull on Monday night, and that she had for many years cohabited with a man residing in Edgar Street, to whom she had had several children. It was also ascertained that she had been an inmate of the Hull Borough Asylum. The poor woman was handed over to the parish officer and has since been conveyed to Clifton Asylum. JULY 1866

HORSE POISONING — During the past week Mr. Thos. North, farmer, of Eske, has lost a valuable horse from the effects of poisoning, others belonging to him being in a precarious position. The loss is supposed to have been the result of the reprehensible practice of administering drugs in the horses' food by the men to improve their appearance. A man employed on the farm was summoned for the offence last Saturday before the East Riding Justices and remanded till today. Mr. North lost several horses from a similar cause two or three years ago. APRIL 1867

THE WEATHER — The past week has been most favourable for haymaking, and the work has been prosecuted with briskness. Yesterday the town crier proclaimed aloud in the streets that mowers were wanted. JULY 1867

CHASE AFTER A PRISONER — On Wednesday evening pedestrians in the neighbourhood of Register Square were somewhat startled at seeing a man at great speed, with four police officials in full cry after him, turn the corner into Toll Gavel and disappear up Walkergate by way of prison pump. On enquiry, it appeared that a young fellow had been apprehended for robbery at Mr. Puckering's, coach builder, and taken to the police office. Here he was examined by the Superintendent and ordered to be locked up; but, just as the officer in charge was reaching the key of the cell, the prisoner bolted like a shot out of the place. Supt. Hopkinson, Inspector McIntosh, and P.C.'s Laughton and Bailey at once set off in pursuit, and, although he managed to get some 30 or 40 yards start, Laughton was at his elbow by the time he reached the Wesleyan day school. Here a row of wood railings barred their progress, but they leaped them together, and, on reaching the ground, the runaway was knocked over a gooseberry bush by the officer and at once collared. He was taken back to the police office and secured in a manner that prevented any further adventure of the kind. FEBRUARY 1868

STAG AT LARGE — During the past week a stag has been at large in Figham, and from the frequency seen at one of the plantations there is supposed to have found a plant of which it is fond. Several attempts to capture it have been made but they have been as ineffectual as they have been ludicrous, the stag having crossed the river repeatedly and so cut off the communication with its would-be captors. It is a truant from the herd at Burton Constable Park. FEBRUARY 1868

OBSTRUCTION — John Waldron, labourer, charged on the 18th *ult.*, with having obstructed the footway in Toll Gavel, by carrying a gate on his shoulders, was fined 1s. and 7s.6d. costs. JANUARY 1869

EXTRAORDINARY EGG — We were shown yesterday an egg laid by a goose belonging to Mr. Thos. Potts of Arram, farmer, which weighed 11 ounces. It measured 12 inches in circumference round the ends and 9 inches round the thickest part. MARCH 1868
(Ouch!)

CHILD DESERTION — On Saturday evening a fine healthy female child apparently two or three weeks old was left in the care of a little girl in East Gate by a woman with a shawl over her head, who stated that she would return immediately. She failed to so do and the child was taken to the police office and from thence to the workhouse. It was not dressed in very respectable clothing. The owner has not been found. MARCH 1869

THE *AURORA BOREALIS.* — A magnificent display of the *Aurora Borealis* was visible on Thursday night between ten and twelve o'clock.
(Aurora Borealis *is more usually known as the Northern Lights.*) MAY 1869

USING THREATENING AND INSULTING LANGUAGE — William Wilson, pot hawker, was charged by Susannah Foster, married woman, of Coxton's Yard, with having on Tuesday, the 25th *ult.* used insulting and disgusting language to her calculated to promote a breach of the peace. The evidence is unfit for publication. The chairman severely admonished the defendant and ordered him to enter into his own recognizance of £20, and find two sureties in £10 each, to keep the peace for six months. JUNE 1869

(What a pity the evidence wasn't published. I would be curious to know if the language then was better or worse than it is now.)

WILFUL DAMAGE — An old offender — Ann Read, a miserable looking object, was brought up on remand, charged with breaking five panes of glass, in the window of Mr. J. Turnbull, of the Queen's Head Public House, Wednesday Market, on Friday last. The prisoner had deliberately smashed the glass with a brick end which she had concealed beneath her shawl. It appears that she had been confined six times in the Beverley House of Correction, twelve times at Wakefield, seven times at Leeds, besides having been imprisoned at Northallerton and Folkingham. The Bench committed her for two months. OCTOBER 1869

(But where this time?)

A DANGEROUS LARK — John Jobson, a lad ten years of age, was charged with having on the 25th April thrown an hedge stake at a passing train from Market Weighton to Beverley from a bridge near to the Kipling Cotes Station. The weapon, it seems, struck the top of one of the carriages. Prisoner pleaded guilty, and it was stated that this was not the first time he and others had amused themselves in that way, the defendant having on a previous occasion thrown a brick at a passing train. A clerk from the office of Mr. Hawkins, the Superintendent of the Railway Police, attended to prosecute and produced Acts of Parliament on the subject. The Bench severely admonished the defendant and inflicted the minimum penalty of 40s. and the costs 9s. The father of the lad, on being asked how he could pay, said he did not know, he having six children besides the defendant. The Bench adjourned the case for a fortnight in order that the case might be represented to the Railway Company, to see if they felt disposed to mitigate the penalty. MAY 1870

THE CASE OF THROWING A STAKE AT A TRAIN — John Jobson, aged ten, the lad who was convicted in the penalty of 40s. and costs for throwing a hedge stake at a passing train from a bridge near Kipling Cotes Station at this court two or three weeks ago, now appeared with his father to hear whether the company had felt disposed to mitigate the penalty in consideration of the parent's position in life. A representative for the company was in attendance and informed the Bench that, the circumstances of the father being taken into account, the company were willing to mitigate the penalty to one of 5s. This sum, together with the costs, amounting in all to 14s., was paid.   MAY 1870

PERAMBULATION — On Monday last was observed the old custom of beating the bounds of St. Martin's parish. The churchwardens, with the clerk, sexton, vestry clerk, and a large retinue of children left the Minster about ten o'clock in the forenoon, and visited the boundary stones of the parish. The Rev. Robert Birtwhistle and Mr A. Birtwhistle accompanied them in their peregrinations. On route, money, *etc.* was scrambled amongst the children, and an unflagging interest kept up by them during the whole of the journey. In Figham buns were distributed to the company, whose appetites were well whetted by their lengthened walk. On returning home, Mr. T. Straker, of the Hall Garth, caused to be scrambled for by the children, in accordance with a custom usually adopted by him on such occasions, a bag full of farthings. The churchwardens and officials afterwards sat down to an excellent dinner provided by Mr. Straker.

MAY 1870

DISGUSTING CONDUCT — Jonas Taylor, labourer, charged with having on Sunday evening wilfully and obscenely exposed his person to two females near to Westwood, was committed to the House of Correction for

three months. — James Hutton, boilermaker, charged with having been drunk and exposed himself in East Gate, the previous night, was fined 10s., including costs.   JULY 1870

(Interesting to note the punishments for what appear to have been similar offences. In the first case two females witnessed that event, but who saw the second case? Probably the fact that he was drunk may have made the difference!)

THROWING DOWN A NEIGHBOUR'S CLOTHESLINE — Hannah Wilson, of Cuttle's Yard, hawker, better known as 'Muffin Hannah', was summoned by Anne Wilkinson, a neighbour, for damaging her clothesline to the amount of 1s., on Friday, the 10th *inst.* Complainant stated that she hung her clothes out to dry, and the defendant broke down the line, let the clothes fall on the ground, and then threw a bucket of water into the yard so as to splash upon them. The defendant, who caused considerable amusement in court by the erratic way in which she conducted her case, said that she had a great washing of her own, and, because the complainant would not take her clothes in to let her dry hers, she threw the prop down. The Bench ordered her to pay 1s., the amount of the damage, and the costs, 5s., or be sent to prison for seven days. The money was eventually paid.   MARCH 1871

NARROW ESCAPE FROM DROWNING — On Monday last a lad named Robson, whose parents reside in Friars Lane, had a very narrow escape from drowning in the Beck. It seems that he was playing with another lad with a rope, and amongst other things they tied it in a knot. They then each took hold of an end to tighten it, when either by accident or from mischief the other lad let go his end and Robson fell into the Beck. A workman, whose name we did not hear, put on the lifebuoy which is near the place and managed to seize the lad after he had sunk twice. The two were then pulled out by Mr. Fisher, manure merchant, and others who happened to be present. The boy, Robson, we believe, was none the worse for his immersion.   JULY 1871

VIOLENT HAIL STORM — On Sunday afternoon last, between three and four o'clock, this town was visited by a hail storm of unusual violence. For several minutes large stones came down with a force that did considerable damage to crops and glass, but we have not heard of any loss of a very serious nature being sustained except to the owners of gardens. The north and east parts of the town seem to have been most affected. In some parts of Westwood it is stated no hail fell, and at Molescroft it does not appear to have been felt so severely as in the town proper. At Leconfield, we believe, it was not felt. The quantity of hail that fell was immense and in some places it was several inches deep. Indeed, we are assured that barrowloads were to be seen in the neighbourhood of the Iron and Waggon Company's works on Monday morning in parts where it had drifted.   AUGUST 1871

SMALLPOX — There have been two deaths from the disease during the past week in Beverley. There are four cases, we believe, in the workhouse, but the sufferers are convalescent; otherwise, we understand, the town is pretty clear of the disease.   MARCH 1872

CRIME IN BEVERLEY

The Superintendent of Police for the Borough, Mr. H. Knight, has reported to the magistrates that the number of summary convictions, within his jurisdiction during the year ending 1st July, 1871, was 261. Of this number 108 were proceeded against for drunkenness, eleven of whom had been previously convicted. For the year ending 1st July, 1872, the returns were as follows:—

Assaults, common 24
Assaults on Police Constables 2
Cruelty to animals 1
Contagious Diseases Act 10
Drunkenness and drunk and disorderly (none
previously convicted the same year) 94
Deserting army 3
Breaches of peace 9
Begging 8
Other offences under Vagrant Act 2
Disorderly conduct in Union 1
Masters and Servants Act 1
Larceny and attempts to steal 13
Malicious and wilful damage 10
Frauds 1
Offence by licensed victualler 1
Beerhouse keeper 1
Hawkers and Pedlars Act 3
Nuisance Removal Act 1
Town Clauses Act 6
Vaccinations Act 2

                                                          ———
                                                          193

These figures show a decrease of 68 as compared with those of the preceding year.   SEPTEMBER 1872

The brilliant fall of meteors on Wednesday evening were seen to advantage by many people in this town.   NOVEMBER 1872

MORE SHEEP WORRYING — During the past week a Leicester ewe belonging to Mr. J. Stamford was worried in a field near to the New Walk. The Guardian Society have offered a reward in order to discover the owner of the dogs.   DECEMBER 1872

KNOCKING FISH ABOUT — Thomas Jobson was summoned at the instance of Peter Harrison Chadwick, fishmonger, for having committed damage to some fish by throwing it about. Complainant stated that the defendant had promised to pay the damage, and he therefore did not wish to press the charge. The Bench allowed it to be withdrawn on defendant paying what was required.   FEBRUARY 1873
(*A definite case of assault and batter(y).*)

DEFACING PAINT — At the Police Court on Monday a man named Smurthwaite was charged with defacing the front of Mr. Brigham's house in Register Square by scratching it. This nuisance of people defacing fronts as soon as they are painted is becoming so common that the police are instructed to take proceedings against offenders. In this instance Mr. Brigham, who was on the Bench, did not wish to press the case, and the man was discharged with a caution, the Bench intimating that persons brought before them on a similar charge would be punished.   MAY 1873

(Even graffiti isn't new!)

REMAINS OF THE MAMMOTH — A few days ago during some excavations for marling purposes on the farm of Mr. Watson, of Biel Beck, near Market Weighton some teeth and other remains of the extinct mammoth were found. Such discoveries in this neighbourhood are, we believe, very rare. Some of the teeth — which are of immense size — are in the possession of Mr. Watson, apprentice to Mr. C. Hobson, druggist of this town.   JUNE 1873

A DIRTY DUCKING — Yesterday morning a lad twelve years of age, who gave the name of Frank Dobson and said his father was a brass finisher residing in Sykes Street, Hull, was fished out of the sewer in Hell Garth Lane and taken to the police station, where he was washed and supplied with breakfast and clean clothes by J. Brigham, Esq. The little fellow had walked from Hull to the races, stayed all night in the town, and was playing with some other lads when he met with his misfortune. Having been made comfortable he was sent home again.   JUNE 1874

(It's that sewer again.)

THE POLICEMEN'S CLOTHING — The following report from the Watch Committee was confirmed on the motion of the Mayor, seconded by Mr. F. Denton: 'This being the usual time for renewing the policemen's great coats, the Committee have accepted the tender of Mr. Bartle for nine coats at £2.8s. and one for the Superintendent at £3.'   OCTOBER 1874

DASTARDLY CONDUCT — Last night week some person cut one of the reins attached to the horse yoked to Mr. Barnes' omnibus whilst it was standing at the Railway Station. A reward of £5 is offered by the Guardian Society for such information as will lead to the conviction of the offender.
FEBRUARY 1875

A FEROCIOUS BEVERLEY COW — At the Hull County Court on Saturday a woman named Turner, who claimed £50 damages for injuries received from a 'savage, wild and ferocious cow', was awarded £15 and costs. The cow had been sold by Mr. Fitzgerald of Beverley to Mr. Keddy of Hull, and Robert Baxter, the man who fetched it, said he was unable to hold it. It ran along the streets and round the Minster and stood on the steps. On arriving with it at Hull it rushed at the plaintiff, threw her up, and stamped upon her, and she received such injuries as compelled her to be placed in the hands of medical men for six weeks. It seemed that the cow was a 'shy' one and ought to have been led by an halter, which Baxter had not done. MARCH 1875

Seldom has there been such a dearth of local news as during the past week. The Borough magistrates have had nothing to do, and scarcely a single incident has occurred in the town worth chronicling. We may at any rate congratulate ourselves upon an absence of crime and casualty, even if there has been inactivity in other matters. MAY 1875

FLOODS IN BEVERLEY — The heavy rain that fell on Monday afternoon flooded the town in several parts. The Market Place was like a pond for an hour or two, with water deep enough to have swum a boat. In Norwood, Mill Lane, and other parts of the town the road in parts was several inches deep, and in some places simply impassable. At the Friary, the home occupied by the Misses Whiteing was inundated to that extent that the furniture had to be removed to a higher room. The water rose to the height of several inches, a circumstance that has never occurred within the memory of the present inhabitants, who were born there. It is supposed that the filling up of the open drain in Hall Garth Lane and the substitution of pipes had to do with the flooding. The latter, not being capable of taking the water off quick enough, had caused it to rush back through the grating in the neighbourhood. Other houses, we understand, besides the Friary were in a similar predicament. AUGUST 1875

WINDOW ACCIDENT — The plate glass window of the Bible Society's Depot, Butcher Row, was broken the other day by a cow running its head into it. AUGUST 1877
(A Sacred Cow?)

DEFACING A WALL — CAUTION TO SCRIBBLERS — Richard Tweedy, tanner, was charged with committing damage to the wall of John Brigham, Esq., of Toll Gavel, by defacing it with writing. Thomas Nelson, a witness, stated that on Saturday morning he saw the defendant write, 'This house to let', on Mr. Brigham's outer wall. P.C. Vary went up at the time and discovered who the offender was. — Daniel Harland, Mr. Brigham's groom, said the wall would have to be painted over again as the writing could not be rubbed off and the cost would be two or three shillings. He had to wash the wall every week on account of mischief of the kind. The defendant pleaded that he was fresh at the time. The Mayor said that this kind of thing must be put a stop to, and defendant would have to pay a fine of 30s., including costs. SEPTEMBER 1877
(If this was the same Mr. Brigham as reported in the 1873 graffiti case, what did the artists have against the poor chap?)

ANNOYING A PARENT — Robert Blyth was summoned but did not appear to answer the charge of having used threatening and abusive language to his mother, Mary Blyth, whereby she considered her life to be in danger. The defendant, she said, went home on Thursday morning after having been out all night and demanded that his breakfast should be at once got ready for him. He then commenced breaking pots and smashing windows and threatened to kill all in the house. He spent all the money he earned in drink and frequently conducted himself in this violent manner. It was stated that when he got the summons he threw it into the fire with an oath. The Bench made an order that he should find sureties for his good behaviour for six months or be imprisoned for one month.

JANUARY 1878

ST. MARY'S SOUP KITCHEN — This institution, which has been the means of doing a large amount of good, is now closed for the winter season. Dinners for the sick and poor will continue to be distributed as usual.

APRIL 1878

A NARROW ESCAPE — In going his rounds on Thursday morning, P.C. Major saw smoke issuing from the engine-house of Mr. E. Fisher's chemical manure works, Beckside. He climbed a wall and broke a window, when he found a heap of coals on fire. He procured some water and soon extinguished the flames, which might speedily have spread and done great damage.

MAY 1879

DISGRACEFUL CONDUCT — Grace Livesey, an abandoned-looking woman, was charged with disorderly conduct the previous night. P.C. Major stated that complaints were made that the prisoner had been in Mr. Wylie's Lane with a number of young men. He took her into custody, and

she was very disorderly on the way to the station and after she was locked up. The Mayor said she would have to go to Hull gaol for a month.
(Tut, Tut!) JUNE 1879

TREAT TO WORKPEOPLE — The men in the employ of Mr. Lowther, coal merchant, of Crane Hill, with their wives, were treated to Bridlington on Tuesday by their employer, who also provided a sumptuous dinner and refreshments for them. The party numbering sixteen very much enjoyed themselves. AUGUST 1879

DAMAGING A BICYCLE — At the Howden Petty Sessions, on Saturday, before Mr. R. S. Schofield and the Hon. A. F. Wood, Thomas Dent, horse dealer, was charged with doing damage to a bicycle, to the extent of 7s., on the Tuesday in Howden Fair week. It was proved that he had thrown a stick at the bicycle whilst it was being propelled, thus capsizing it, whereby it sustained damage as above-named. Defendant appeared in court in a state of semi-intoxication, and his defence at times excited, and at others ridiculous and rambling, was to the effect that he had merely thrown the stick for fun and with no intention of damaging the machine. He was fined, however, 10s. and costs and ordered to pay the amount claimed.
(Sounds more like a boat than a bicycle.) OCTOBER 1879

BANK HOLIDAY — Yesterday, being the Christmas Bank Holiday, most of the shops and places of business in the town were closed. The weather was fine but it was intensely cold, and skating seemed to be one of the chief sources of out-door amusements. DECEMBER 1879

THE VICTORIA BARRACKS — The decorations for the season at the Barracks were of a lavish description, and Christmas Day was enjoyed in a thoroughly English way. In the evening a dance was held, and the company, which was very large, kept it up with much spirit. DECEMBER 1879
(Was there something in the drink?)

NARROW ESCAPE FROM RAILWAY ACCIDENT — Three little children named Lazenby had a hairsbreadth escape from being run over on Monday morning last near the Beverley Railway Station. They attempted to cross the line just as the 9.55 train to Hull had left, and did not notice the train arriving from Hull at the same time. One of the boys was so near that he touched the engine. Some spectators were aghast when they saw the impending danger and considered it next to a miracle that the children had escaped. FEBRUARY 1880

ANNOYING THE ROMAN CATHOLIC PRIEST — A lad was brought before the Borough magistrates on Monday charged with annoying the Rev. T. A. Smith. The latter had written a letter to the Bench complaining strongly of the conduct of lads who annoyed him by ringing his bell and in other ways. It was alleged that the lad in court had pushed Mr. Smith's servant down, broken a jug and wasted some milk it contained. — The Bench ordered the lad's mother to pay the girl 6d. for the jug and the milk and to give her son a good thrashing. MARCH 1880

(I hope he got his deserved thrashing, the bad lad.)

WANTON MISCHIEF — On Saturday night or Sunday morning last a new seat which had just been placed at the pitheads in Westwood was torn up and thrown into the bushes. Its size and weight was such that it must have taken several persons to remove it. The Pasture Masters have offered a reward of £2 for the discovery of the offenders, and we sincerely hope they will succeed in finding them and prosecute them when they do so.

JUNE 1880

DEDICATION OF A CHURCH BELL — A fine old bell, procured from one of the Norwich churches, which has just been hung in St. Nicholas' church tower by Mr. Malloby of Boroughbridge was dedicated on Sunday morning last. A special service was held at seven o'clock, when the bell was dedicated to the service of God by the rector, The Hon. and Rev. F. G. Pelham. The choir sang appropriate hymns in the tower and the churchyard. The Rev. C. G. Nation, and Mr. Brodrick, the architect, were amongst those present. MAY 1881

The pallisades which surrounded the obelisk in Wednesday Market have been removed, and workmen are engaged in taking down the obelisk, which is to be superseded by an ornamental lamp. DECEMBER 1881

The new ornamental lamp in Wednesday Market, which is fitted with a patent burner and reflector, was lighted yesterday for the first time. DECEMBER 1881

DAMAGE BY LIGHTNING — During the storm which took place on Saturday night last the Register House was struck by the electric fluid, and one of the bedrooms and its contents were almost entirely destroyed. Those of the inmates who had not retired to rest were naturally very much alarmed, but they did not sustain any injury. Had the bedroom been tenanted at the time, the consequences would have been most serious. DECEMBER 1881

THE COST OF LUNACY TO THE BEVERLEY UNION — At the fortnightly meeting of the Board of Guardians held on Saturday D. Burton, Esq., the chairman, drew attention to the amount which it had cost for the maintenance of pauper lunatics belonging to the Union. The sum was £253.3s.0d. for the quarter, being at the rate of more than £1,000 a year. A part of it, he remarked, was paid back by the government, but it came out of the pockets of the ratepayers in one way or another. He believed the fact of the Asylum being so near to the Union was one reason why they had so many patients in the institution. He had noticed that when they received testimonials from applicants for the office of medical superintendent that it was the same in other places. In reply to a Guardian the chairman said the amount received from the government was 4s. per head and each patient cost 9s.11d. per head. JANUARY 1882

SEASONABLE BENEVOLENCE — Sir James Walker, Bart., of the Hall, Beverley, and Sand Hutton, has instructed Mr. John Lowther to distribute, for the fifth time this season, a quantity of coals amongst the poor of St. Martin's parish, which, considering that there is considerable distress existing, and the weather having set in severe, will no doubt be gratefully received. FEBRUARY 1882

THE BEVERLEY IRON AND WAGGON WORKS — The buildings, materials, hammer, furnace chimneys etc., constituting what was left of the above works, were disposed of by auction by Mr. Norfolk on Wednesday and Thursday last. It is said that a large quantity of the materials was purchased by the Corporation who intend to build a new corn exchange.

SEPTEMBER 1882

LAUNCH OF AN IRON VESSEL AT BEVERLEY — Whatever position the town may ultimately attain as a ship building mart, it has, at any rate, been the good fortune of two Beverlonians — Messrs. Henry and Joseph Scarr — to initiate the work and to be the first to enter upon this particular kind of industry. Messrs. Scarr, it will be remembered, built, and successfully launched, a few weeks ago, an iron vessel which was purchased by Messrs. Crathorne and Sons. This venture probably emboldened them to take an order from Mr. C. M. Jacobs of Cardiff in April last to construct an iron steamer of greater proportions than had hitherto been attempted here. The proportions were as follows:— length over perpendiculars 115 feet; breadth mould 17 feet 9 inches; depth of hold 9 feet. The vessel was ready for launching last Wednesday, when the event had become pretty generally known. Beckside presented such an appearance as it has seldom done before. Hundreds of persons had gathered to see the spectacle. The huge vessel as it stood on the slips looked like causing a tremendous displacement of the water, and there were some present who had fears that the Beck wall might suffer, so little room did there seem for such a large hull to glide into. A few minutes after 3 o'clock, however, the last support was knocked away and the trigger having been cut by the Rev. R. Shepherd, the vessel, amidst enthusiastic cheers, slid into the water (sideways) and righted herself in a moment, settling down quietly into midstream. As she was loosed from the slips she was named *Alice* by Miss Annie Scarr, daughter of one of the partners.

NOVEMBER 1882

(No doubt the launch of an iron vessel must have been a wondrous thing — especially to see it floating!)

SPURIOUS COIN — We understand that a number of counterfeit sovereigns and half sovereigns have been circulated in the town during the past week. As they are excellent imitations tradesmen are cautioned to be on the alert.

JUNE 1883

ANNOYANCE BY THE SALVATION ARMY — At the Guildhall, on Monday, Superintendent Knight reported to the magistrates that he had received several complaints respecting the Salvation Army. On the previous (Sunday) morning they paraded the streets headed by their band soon after six o'clock and the noise aroused nearly all the townspeople. The Mayor said it was exceedingly wrong that people should be disturbed in this way. The other Justices concurred, and the Superintendent was instructed to take out a summons in case of similar annoyance in future.

MARCH 1884

GAMBLERS AT THE RACES — On Thursday the Borough magistrates had before them at the Guild Hall a number of prisoners charged with the above offence. Most of the men came from Leeds and Manchester and they pleaded guilty to the charges. The means employed were the three card trick, spinning jennies, and prick belt. A fine of 40s. was inflicted in each case.   JUNE 1884

TYPHOID EPIDEMIC — *During the summer of 1884 Beverley experienced a serious epidemic of typhoid, causing the death of 18 people — most cases with the disease appeared to originate from the area supplied by water from the new waterworks. Some believed the problem originated in the sewers while others blamed the water supply — the outcome was to indicate that both sources were at fault. However, in a public health report in 1890 it was believed that there had been typhoid cases at Broadgate Hospital (known then as the East Riding Asylum) at Walkington, and that sewage from the Asylum had been discharged onto a field near to the waterworks and seaped through into the water supply. For many weeks the* Beverley Guardian *carried correspondence at great length on the subject and some people even reported their own findings on the state of the water, after having private analysis carried out on samples, in the August 9 edition under a heading, 'What was not told at the Council meeting'. We have included some of the questions asked in an attempt to solve the cause of the outbreak:*

'How it was that some of the public sewers were cleaned out at an early hour in the morning, and afterwards inspected by the civil engineer appointed by the Sanitary Committee to make an enquiry?'

'Why water was taken surreptitiously for the purpose of analysis from a fire pipe in St. Mary's Church, which had not been opened out for weeks?'

'Why, when it was found in opening out the drain in Keld Gate, and in searching for a leakage in the water pipes in Walkergate, that the ground was saturated with sewage that nothing was said about it by the Sanitary Committee in their report?'   AUGUST 1884
Eventually improvements were made to the sanitary system and waterworks after a costly lesson in lives had been learnt.)

TRIBUTE TO AN OLD FRIEND — A gentleman, a bachelor of the town, having recently lost by death a favourite cat, which for twenty-seven years has been his trusty friend, gave it a burial the other day which seldom falls to the lot of one of the feline race. A substantial coffin was provided and it was placed along with the body of a bottle containing the history of poor pussy. It was then decently and carefully interred in the owner's garden.

                                                                    OCTOBER 1884

A DANGEROUS PRACTICE — Three lads named Parks, Brooks and Fitzgerald, were ordered to appear before the Borough magistrates on Monday to answer the charge of throwing a lighted cracker into the shop of Mr. James Sherwood, of Lairgate, on the night of the 1st *instant*. The Bench pointed out the danger there was in such conduct, and ordered the lads to appear next Monday, their behaviour to be considered in the meantime.

                                                                  NOVEMBER 1884

RIDING ON THE RAILWAY WITHOUT A TICKET — Thomas Botterill, barman, was summoned for having on the 12th February last travelled between Beverley and Hull without a ticket with intent to defraud the railway company. Inspector Kemp of the North Eastern Railway Police attended to prosecute and he stated the case. Defendant admitted the offence, and no witnesses were therefore called. The Bench fined him 40s. and 9s.6d. costs or one month's imprisonment.   MAY 1885

ATTACKED BY A BULL — On Thursday a man named Dunning in the employ of Mr. Robert Sugden at his farm in Beverley Parks was attacked by a bull and badly injured. The infuriated animal, after knocking him into a ditch and butting him severely in different parts of the body, left him. He is now under the care of Mr. Calvert, at his home in Friar's Lane.

                                                                       MAY 1885

THE SUGGESTED NEW CORN EXCHANGE BUILDINGS — The Property Committee of the Council have had submitted to them nineteen designs for a new Corn Exchange, Baths and Butter Market. Four of them have been selected for the consideration of the Council next Monday.

                                                               SEPTEMBER 1885
(*The design selected was the one presented by architect Samuel Musgrave.*)

ALLEGED IMPROPER TRAVELLING OF A LOCOMOTIVE —
Ralph Keddy, locomotive owner, Lund, was summoned for an infraction of
the Act, by not having a man walking in front of his engine, at Lockington,
on the 18th November. P.C. Clarkson said he saw no one in front, but a
witness was called who swore that he walked about 30 yards in advance of
it all the way from Lund to Lockington. The Bench, after hearing the
evidence, dismissed the case.   DECEMBER 1885
(*With a red flag, I hope!*)

NEW FIRE ENGINE — Superintendent Knight has accepted the tender
of Messrs. Merryweather of London to supply one of their Gold Medal
manual engines for the Beverley Fire Brigade. The engine, which may be
worked by 36 men, will be capable of throwing 156 gallons of water per
minute, will cost £136, and £9 more will be required for additional hose and
payment of other expenses.   JANUARY 1886

VALENTINE DAY — There was a considerable falling off in the
Valentine trade this year, so much so that the ordinary business of the Post
Office was not interefered with and the delivery on Sunday morning took
place within an hour of the ordinary time.   FEBRUARY 1886

THE QUEEN'S BIRTHDAY — In honour of this event the depot of the
15th Regiment met on parade on Saturday morning last and gave hearty
cheers for the Queen.   JUNE 1886
(*Happy Birthday, Ma'am.*)

DISTRICT INTELLIGENCE — Dalton Holme. Lord Hotham was a prize taker (with grapes) at the floral exhibition held in connection with the Yorkshire gala this week, and Mr. Alsopp, his lordship's gardener, was one of the judges of pelargoniums, roses, and cut flowers at the same show.
JUNE 1886

THE NEW CORN EXCHANGE — We have deferred our account of this building until completion of the baths, *etc.*, which are rapidly progressing. We may state, however, that to meet the engagements of the past week, the surveyor, Mr. Sharpe, the gas manager, Mr. Bryan, and the contractors, Messrs. Pape, have been most assiduous in their efforts to make available the Corn Exchange and the Butter Market, and in this they have been successful.
NOVEMBER 1886

(The reader may be interested to know that on the day that the new Corn Exchange opened, November 24, the Beverley Ornithological Society held a Grand Exhibition of Birds accompanied by music and singing. The Public Baths which formed the other part of the Corn Exchange/Baths complex did not open until April 4, 1887, but we have decided to include the report given of the event.)

THE CORPORATION BATHS — These baths, which form part of the new Corn Exchange and Butter Market buildings, were opened without any ceremony on Monday morning last. The same evening 117 lads availed themselves of the advantages thus offered them by patronising the swimming baths.
APRIL 1887

ROAD SAFETY
(or Road User Offences)

The motor car was still a long way off when this episode starts. It's the day of horses, carts and stable manure on the road, long before the days of 'Blow in here, please, sir.' But the danger of being drunk in charge was very much in evidence and you still 'got done' for it. In this episode you will gasp in amazement at the reports of furious riding and furious driving and the sad case of the horse and cart left unattended. PHR

CAUTION TO WAGGONERS — Henry Trowell was summoned at the instance of Superintendent Pattison for allowing a quantity of stable manure to be scattered from his vehicle which was proceeding along North Bar Street whereby he had rendered himself liable to a penalty of £2. The charge was admitted by the defendant, who was ordered to pay the expenses.

NOVEMBER 1862

(This reminded me of the day my father sent me into the street, red-faced and armed with bucket and shovel — 'Good for the roses,' he said.)

FURIOUS RIDING — William Juby was charged with being drunk and riding in a reckless manner along Toll Gavel whereby the safety of the public was endangered and three persons narrowly escaped serious injury, between six and seven o'clock the previous evening. The animal, soon after turning the corner of Register Square, fell, and the drunken fellow rolled off. He was fined 10s. including costs, or in default 14 days' imprisonment.

APRIL 1863

A NICE PAIR — William Shaw, who did not appear but was represented by his better half, was charged with leaving his horse and cart in the street for about four hours without anyone in charge of the same on Tuesday, the 21st of February, the owner and his wife being drunk in a public house. It was further stated that defendant gave the police a great deal of trouble, as scarcely a week passed without his horse and cart standing in the street while he was drinking in a public house. Fined 15s. including costs.

(We wouldn't say they were a nice pair.)   MARCH 1865

SCATTERING MANURE — Peter Parker, labourer, was charged with leading manure during prohibited hours, to wit, at ten o'clock on the previous morning. It seemed that manure was dropping from the defendant's cart. The case was proved by H. Barkworth Esq. and Sergt.

Steel. Defendant said he had been at the work since four o'clock in the morning and that was his last load. The Bench fined him 10s. including costs, and intimated that the next offence would be visited with the full penalty.   MAY 1874

(Just fancy that! Prohibited hours for leading manure!)

DRIVING WITHOUT REINS — A youth named Johnson was summoned for driving in a cart without having proper control over his horses. He admitted it, and said he had got into the cart because he did not feel well. The Bench did not convict, his master having given him a good character, but simply ordered him to pay the costs, 6s.   APRIL 1881

FURIOUS DRIVING — Charles Swailes, horse dealer, was charged with being drunk and disorderly and also with furious driving. It seems that the prisoner with horse and cart had driven about the fair on Monday, and had run against the Custom House Vaults *[an inn at the corner of Ladygate]* with great violence. He and a companion alighted from the cart to get more drink, and he was apprehended by Sergeant Robson for being drunk and disorderly. The Bench fined him 40s. and 16s.6d. costs.   JULY 1886

THEFT
THOU SHALT NOT STEAL
BUT THEY DID

And just what would you think they stole? Forget the videos, T.V.s and cars. There were none of those around so our friends of those bygone days 'nicked' such things as eggs, beans, ducks, crabs, soot and bones — the list is endless. But what about the chap who was caught near the poultry with a bag? Was he after a chicken or droppings? Then there were those two young lads who couldn't resist the temptation to steal a couple of night shirts — well, they had 'sort of' found them in a field. But these lads were no fools: they 'tore them to shreds' and then sold them for one penny. Their punishment? All will be revealed with this episode along with many other exciting escapades! PHR/PAH

73

George Sider, labourer, was charged with stealing eggs from his master, Mr. Richard Todd of Eske, and sentenced to six weeks' imprisonment.
AUGUST 1856

James Dixon and Margaret Wood remanded on suspicion of stealing bones were today discharged, no owner being found for the property.
JANUARY 1857

Henry Boyle was brought up in custody charged with stealing a pair of sheets, the property of Mrs. Sutheran, a lodging-house keeper in this town, on the 30th *ult.* Twenty-one days' imprisonment.
FEBRUARY 1857

Richard Wilson (38), and Richard Wright (27), sweeps, were charged with stealing at Holme-on-Spalding Moor two quarters of soot, the property of Henry Ward. Prosecutor, a farmer, had 40 quarters of soot, which he engaged the prisoners to sow on three of his fields, who, after hiding two full bags in a ditch, took them away. Both were found guilty. A previous conviction being proved against Wilson, he was sentenced to four years' penal servitude, and Wright to three months' imprisonment.   JULY 1858

Thomas Jones of Beverley was charged with being found in an outhouse belonging to Mr. Leaper on the previous night under suspicious circumstances, he having with him a bag and being near some poultry. Defendant had been a ticket-of-leave man, and was sent to prison for two months.   OCTOBER 1858

PLEADED GUILTY — Catherine Grady (50) widow, to stealing a shawl on the 3rd of November, the property of Jane Whitehead of Beverley. Mr. Peel prosecuted. A previous conviction having been proved against her, she, for the second time, received sentence of four years' penal servitude.
JANUARY 1860

£3 REWARD — Beverley Guardian Society for the Prosecution of Felons and Protection of Trade. WHEREAS some person or persons, during the last week, entered a field situate on the east side of Bogle Lane *[now Beaver Road)* in Beverley, occupied by Mr. William Watson, of Minster Moorgate, and feloniously stole therefrom EIGHT RAILS and THE GATE LOCK, and broke about forty tiles on the roof of his shed, NOTICE IS HEREBY GIVEN that a reward of three pounds will be paid by this society to any person who shall give such information to me as will lead to the conviction of the offender or offenders.

By order of the Committee,
  JOHN BLYTHE ROBINSON,
    Solicitor to the Society.   MARCH 1860

John Ward, blacksmith, from Huddersfield, was brought up on remand, charged with stealing a kidney from the shop board of Mr. John Flower, butcher, Butcher Row. The prisoner pleaded guilty, and was sentenced to two months' imprisonment.   MARCH 1862

Thomas Addy, another juvenile, was charged with stealing a quantity of beans, on Sunday, the 10th *instant*, from a stack in Beverley Parks belonging to Mr. Thomas Denton. The defendant, on being detected, ran away, and, on being overtaken, his pockets were found to be full of beans. He was admonished and discharged.   MARCH 1862

STEALING COAL — Ellen Taylor, widow, pleaded guilty to stealing, on Friday morning last, four stones weight of coal from the yard of Mr. James Scruton, coal dealer, Beckside, and was committed to the House of Correction for seven days.   OCTOBER 1868

CHARGE OF STEALING TOBACCO — Patrick Myers, a tramp, was brought up charged with having on the previous day stolen two half ounces of tobacco from the shop of Mr. Marshall, chemist and druggist, Toll Gavel. Prisoner was remanded till Monday next.   FEBRUARY 1872

ROBBING A MUSICIAN — At the Hull Police Court, on Thursday, Charles S. McDonald, brought up on remand, charged with stealing two clarinets, the property of Mr. Isaac Gray, of Beverley, and a musician at the Theatre Royal, Hull, was again remanded for eight days.   MARCH 1872

ROBBERY BY A SERVANT — Jane Taylor, a girl about thirteen years of age, was brought up charged with stealing a number of trifling articles, the property of Robert Haldenby, keeper of the Royal Oak beerhouse, Westwood Road, Keldgate, with whom she lived as a servant. The property, which consisted of tea, cigars, pocket handkerchiefs, *etc.*, were missed by the prosecutor, and ultimately found in the prisoner's box. She was apprehended by P.C. Wick on Saturday under a warrant. She now pleaded guilty, and the Mayor, after admonishing her, sentenced her to the light punishment of seven days' imprisonment on account of her youth.
                                                       JANUARY 1873

ARTFUL LADS — Frederick Usher, aged 10, and George Witty, aged 9, were charged with stealing two calico night gowns, the property of Henry Saunders, from a field where they had been left to dry. The lads had taken the gowns from the lines, torn them in shreds and sold them to a marine store dealer for a penny. They now pleaded guilty, and the Bench ordered them to be locked up for five hours and also to receive ten strokes each from the birch rod, to be administered by Superintendent Wright.

FEBRUARY 1874

CONSCIENCE MONEY — On the clearing of Westwood on the 1st January, Mr. F. Denton, of Railway Street, lost a lamb, value from 20s. to 25s. Since then he has made enquiries in various places without gaining any tidings of the animal. On Wednesday night last, an envelope was put into Mr. Denton's letter-box, containing 22s. worth of postage stamps and a letter, badly spelt, but evidently in a feigned hand. The following is a copy:— 'Sur I send you the price of a lam that I tuk out of Westwoodd mak no queyreys about it cus you no get ta no any mare.' [sic]

FEBRUARY 1874

CHARGE OF STEALING A DUCK — On Monday, William G. of Dog and Duck Lane, labourer, was brought up before R. Wylie Esq., charged with stealing a live duck, the property of Mark Holmes of Arram, farmer, on Saturday night last. The prisoner was remanded till this day, and admitted to bail himself in £20, and surety in £10. *(After appearing before the East Riding Police Court he was sent to prison for one calendar month with hard labour).*

MAY 1874

ALLEGED ROBBERY FROM DWELLING HOUSE — It has been reported to the police that the house of Mr. John Gray, pig jobber, Woodmansey, was entered on Tuesday during the absence of the family at Hull Fair and over £30 taken from under the bed. The police have been unable to discover any marks of housebreaking and the matter at present remains a mystery.

OCTOBER 1874

ROBBING A FELLOW WORKMAN — George Walker, a shoemaker, was charged with stealing a top coat, the property of William Blake. Both parties were working in December for Mr. Sturdy of North Bar Street and a day or two before Christmas Day prisoner took away the coat which he promised to return. He failed to do so and it was subsequently ascertained that he had sold the coat for 1s.3d. on the 30th December to a man in the Sun public house. Prisoner pleaded guilty, and said he had no recollection of selling the coat. He must have done so whilst keeping his Christmas holiday. He said he would give up drinking and become a teetotaller. It seemed that he was apprehended on Saturday by Sergeant Tomlinson at York, where he had just done two months for felony. The Mayor sentenced him to 21 days' hard labour, and prisoner left the court remarking that he had got well over it.   APRIL 1876

A DISSATISFIED GAOL BIRD — At the Guildhall on Thursday before the Mayor and R. G. Boulton, Esq., John Moorish, a tramp, was brought up charged by P.C. Haldenby with stealing a crab from the shop board of Mr. Robert Hodgson, fishmonger, on the previous night. The prisoner was seen to take a crab by a boy and he gave information to Haldenby, who found him eating the crab in North Bar Street. Prisoner, who had been twice before the Bench previously, asked to be convicted for six months. The Mayor committed him for two months. After being sentenced prisoner said if he had known he should only get two months he would have taken five or six crabs. Prisoner subsequently stated that he had been in twenty-six prisons, and there were three he had not been in. He was determined to be in them and then he would go home to Exeter to his friends. APRIL 1876

DAMAGE AND ROBBERY — The Beverley Guardian Society for the Prosecution of Felons and the Protection of Trade have offered a reward of £5 for information which will lead to the discovery of the person or persons who on Saturday night last partly unroofed a shed belonging to Mr. W. Southwick, situate in Cherry Tree Lane, and stole therefrom a quantity of wood.   MAY 1876

CHARGE OF STEALING LEAD FROM THE NEW BARRACKS — At the East Riding Police Court, Beverley, on Saturday, Robert Stewart, a plumber's labourer, who had been employed at the new barracks since last June, was charged with stealing about ten hundredweight of lead, the property of Messrs. Walsh and Son of Halifax, who have the contract for the plumbing work at the barracks. Evidence was given to show that the prisoner had disposed of a quantity of lead, melted down, to William Thompson, marine store dealer, of Beverley, and John Shaw, a metal broker, of Hull, and also that he had been employed at the barracks first by Mr. Barratt, contractor, and latterly by Messrs. Walsh. On the application of Superintendent Naylor the prisoner was remanded till this day.
                                                                 JANUARY 1877

ROBBERY OF CARROTS BY LADS — Several lads, varying from eight to thirteen years of age, were ordered to appear before the Bench to answer the charge of stealing and destroying a quantity of carrots, the property of Mr. Lake, of the railway coal depot. It appeared that they had not only taken the carrots from the garden to eat, but they had strewn them about the road. The Mayor dismissed them with a caution, telling them that the next time they came up on a similar charge they would be sent to prison.
OCTOBER 1880

MORE GARDEN ROBBING — On Monday, at the Police Court, four stable lads from 14 to 18 years of age, named David Turnbull, Charles Lazenby, Anthony Richardson and John Botterill, were charged with stealing apples from the garden of Miss Emily Boulton, of York Terrace. Mr. Hawkins, a neighbour, caught the lads leaving the garden on Sunday, the 4th *inst.* He gave evidence to this effect, but thought the younger lads were entitled to some consideration as they had been led on by the others. Superintendent Knight said he had received numerous complaints of gardens being robbed. Defendants pleaded guilty, and the chairman in fining them 10s. each stated that the Bench in future would send them or others so offending to prison.
SEPTEMBER 1881
(I know it was theft, but when I was a lad it was scrumping, and, if you were caught, a clip or thrashing had a deterrent effect.)

HOUSEBREAKING — James Hebdon, *alias* Fred Archer, a rag and bone gatherer, was charged with breaking into the dwelling house of Mr. Jas. Dawson of Union Road *[now Woodlands]* and stealing a cash box containing valuable securities, six bottles of wine, and other articles. The prisoner was connected with a gang of four others, who have since been apprehended, and will be brought up on Monday next.
NOVEMBER 1881

ROBBING AN EMPLOYER — Henry Kidston, who described himself as a sailor, was charged with stealing a dog, the property of George Johnson of North Newbald, shoemaker, and a shirt and scarf, the property of Timothy Beasley. It appears that the prosecutor, Johnson, who takes harvest work to do, had engaged the prisoner to help him, and he lodged in his house. On getting up one morning prosecutor missed the dog and other articles. Information was given to P.C. Chapman, who apprehended the prisoner. The latter now pleaded guilty. He was committed to gaol for one month with hard labour.
OCTOBER 1882

ROBBERY FROM THE PURSE — At the Guildhall on Monday, Annie Cullen, a girl aged 19, was charged with stealing 13s., the property of William Robinson, umbrella mender. The prosecutor had taken the girl to his house for an improper purpose and while she was there she took the money out of his pocket. He gave information to the police, and P.C.s Prior and Wick went to a house in Kitchen Lane where the prisoner lodged. They found two half crowns and two shillings hid in a kettle and they apprehended the prisoner. She now admitted the charge. Supt. Knight said the prisoner was convicted of a similar offence last November. The Bench under these circumstances, committed her for trial at the Quarter Sessions.

JULY 1886

(*I think it served him right. Improper purpose, indeed. Tut, tut.*)

THEFT OF STOCKINGS — Robert Bannatt, a sailor, was charged with stealing a pair of men's stockings, the property of Mr. Crowson, of Ellerton. Witnesses were called to give evidence in support of the charge, and they stated that on the 13th *inst.* they saw the prisoner take the stockings off a hedge. At the close of the evidence the Justices sentenced the prisoner to 1 month's imprisonment.

JULY 1886

STEALING ROSES — James Everett, labourer, was charged with stealing roses from the garden of Mr. Hudson, of Longcroft, and he admitted the offence. Mr. Hudson, who retired from the Bench, stated that he did not wish to press for heavy punishment as defendant's wife had a large family which she had to support, her husband spending what he earned in drink. Roses had been missed from his garden for the last three weeks. Mr. Hare, the complainant's gardener, said the present offence was committed on the previous Saturday evening, when about twenty roses were taken. — The chairman said the Bench would mitigate the punishment after what Mr. Hudson had said; it was a most grateful act (the complainant had employed him) to do as he had done. He will be fined 1s. and 9s. costs.

AUGUST 1886

TRIVIAL BITS

Most of the entries included in this Trivial Bits collection are literally that, and during research were found to be of sufficient interest to include in the collection. But when the big sort-out came far too many headings were required, so the lazy and easy way came to mind, ' "Trivia", let's stick all those bits of interest etc., under that heading,' and so we did. Here are presented short newsy bits, like 'injuries to grass', 'painting fish', 'The Danger of Orange Peel', a letter from the poor chambermaid and her grumble about the waterworks. PHR

Henry Milner, Frederick Hobson, and John Peck, three juveniles, were summoned at the instance of Mr. George Stephenson for trespassing in his field in Norwood and injuring the grass. Complainant not wishing to press the case, they were discharged on payment of the costs.
FEBRUARY 1857

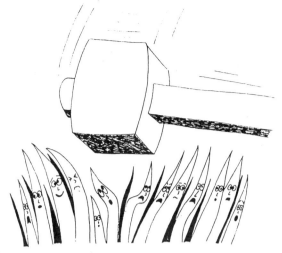

Sarah Ann Beck, an inmate of the workhouse, was brought up under the following circumstances:— Mr. Hudson, the master, stated she was very refractory, and not only refused to work when requested but assaulted her fellow paupers and he was compelled to lock her up in her room, where she broke eleven panes of glass. Committed to prison for 42 days.
FEBRUARY 1857

Sidney Adamson and Ann Merrell, two girls, were charged with obstructing the footway opposite the shop of Mr. Harrison, and on being requested to go away gave him a bountiful supply of abuse. Ordered to pay costs.
APRIL 1857

FOUR RECIPES FOR LAUGHTER — There are four things on the stage which never fail to make an audience laugh, viz:— 1, a woman slapping a man's face; 2, Eating in a hurry, and speaking with your mouth full; 3,

Breaking a plate; and 4, Kicking, 'bonneting', or tickling anybody with a red hot poker; — more especially, if the person so kicked, 'bonneted', or tickled, happens to be a policeman. — *Punch's Pocket Book.*
DECEMBER 1857

PAINTING FISH — The Inspector of Liverpool Fish Market has detected a mode of adulteration in use among fish dealers. A red powder, perhaps poisonous, is sprinkled upon the fish. This, when wet, looks like blood, and gives the fish an appearance of freshness — ('What next?' may well be asked.)
FEBRUARY 1858
(*Yes, what next? Before you know it they will be putting colours in all our foods!*)

CAUTION TO LADS — At the Guildhall on Thursday two boys were brought up in custody charged with obstructing the footpath by playing at marbles on Butterding Flags the previous evening. His Worship gave them a caution and discharged them after giving them to understand that if brought up again for a similar offence they would be punished.
MARCH 1872
(*Would you believe it? Cautioned for playing marbles. It's incredible when you think of what they get away with nowadays.*)

THE DANGER OF ORANGE PEEL — The public are cautioned (by handbill) against throwing orange peel on the pavement on pain of having proceedings taken against them by the police. Considering the great damage

to life and limb likely to ensue from the practice people must be very thoughtless or stupid who continue it. JANUARY 1873
(Could orange peel have been worse than people allowing their dogs to foul the pavements in these times?)

CORRESPONDENCE

WATERWORKS

To the Editor of the *Beverley Guardian.*

Dere Mister Edditer, — I am a chambremade in Bevly and wish ther was watterworks to karry watter upstairs. For me, I am nearly all day breaking my back huggin kans of watter and the pumpin. When I were in Hull we had watter on the landing upstairs and in the Bathroom and Skullry just for turning the tap and for coachman to swill his karridge. Master told us the watter cost him no more as pump out of order in last hous. I will either have my wages ris or go back tif Hull.
CHAMBERMADE *[sic]*
[N.B. — The Editor is not responsible for the spelling.]
NOVEMBER 1878
(Another one of those specials — a must for inclusion.)

AN UNFORTUNATE — Annie Hutton, a respectably dressed girl, only 18 years of age, who stated she came from Grimsby, was charged with vagrancy. P.C. Bailey found her that morning at 12.40 in a shed in Tiger Lane. Two men were in the same building. She was discharged with a caution and advised to leave the town forthwith. MAY 1880

SNOWBALLING NUISANCES — Superintendent Knight informed the Bench at the Borough Police Court on Monday that he had received several complaints of boys throwing snowballs, particularly in respect to ladies and old people. He intimated that he should take out summonses against any who might be reported in the future. JANUARY 1886

CAUTION TO SNOWBALLERS — At the Guildhall on Monday, before the Mayor (Mr. Tom Turner) and Mr. R. Hodgson, Jnr., Robert Tomlinson, and William Hurst, were summoned for throwing a snowball at a young girl named Louisa Simpson on Sunday, 24th *ult*. Defendants were together in North Bar Street and one of them threw a snowball which went through the complainant's umbrella. P.C. Wood stated that he saw the defendants throwing snowballs at different people in Market Place and North Bar Street on the day in question. Defendants admitted the charge. The Mayor said each of them would have to pay 6s. or seven days' imprisonment. Supt. Knight remarked that he had received several complaints of injury done by lads throwing snowballs. One girl had been struck on the face and her eye blackened.   FEBRUARY 1886

CORRESPONDENCE

To the Editor of the *Beverley Guardian*.

Dear Sir, — My attention was drawn on Sunday evening last to about a dozen ladies and gentlemen endeavouring at different doors to get into the Minster during the time the evening service was going on. It was a bitterly cold night and after vainly trying for a long time most of them went away.

It seems to me, Sir, a most outrageous thing that any national church should lock its doors against intending worshippers during the time of public divine service, and I think the congregation themselves cannot surely know that they are locked in a public building — and in case of a panic at the mercy of a sleepy verger — or they would never allow themselves to run such a risk.

Yours truly F.B.   FEBRUARY 1886

SLEEPING OUT — Four tramps were brought up, charged by Sergeant Jackson with having been found in a shed in a field in the occupation of Mr. T. Stephenson in Beverley Parks the previous night without any visible means of subsistence. The were committed to prison for 14 days.

JULY 1886